# Adventures with Chocolate

paul.a.young

# *Adventures* *with* Chocolate

## 80 Sensational Recipes

photography by Anders Schønnemann

Kyle Books

## For Mum
**For your everlasting support, patience and love.**

Published in 2011 by Kyle Books
www.kylebooks.com

Distributed by National Book Network
4501 Forbes Blvd., Suite 200
Lanham, MD 20706
Phone: (800) 462-6420
Fax: (301) 429-5746
custserv@nbnbooks.com

First published in 2009 by Kyle Cathie Limited

ISBN 978-1-906868-05-5

Project editor: Jenny Wheatley
Designer: Carl Hodson
Photographer: Anders Schønnemann
Food Stylist: Annie Rigg
Stylist: Tabitha Hawkins
Copy editor: Emily Hatchwell
Production director: Kyle Cathie

Library of Congress Control Number: 2011926474

Color separations by Sang Choy, Singapore
Printed and bound in China by C&C Offset

*Recipe photographs feature the first recipe on the facing page*

# Contents

# Introduction

**Underslept and bursting with excitement, I rip the festive wrapping paper off the book-sized package and, to my joy, it's a box of Thornton's Continental chocolates.**

It was Christmas Day sometime in the mid-1980s, when I should have been playing with my new Space Invaders game. But I was never any good at, or much interested in, video games. Place a box of the finest chocolates in my lap, however, and I was mesmerized. I should point out that Thornton's Continental were the *haute couture* of chocolates in my home town back then. Needless to say, small villages outside Durham, England, weren't overflowing with artisan patisseries or chocolate shops in those days!

This passion for chocolate and all things sweet stayed with me throughout school and well into my resturant school years, when I managed to get myself placed on the dessert section of the training kitchen most weeks. I tried every way possible to include chocolate in every dessert – even if it was just a delicate decoration or a great big chunk of chocolate brownie or fudge cake.

I finally landed a dream job as a trainee pastry chef at London's Criterion Brasserie, domain of Marco Pierre White. I relished the new smells and textures, the kitchen French and, of course, the chocolate. We used Valrhona chocolate, which I had heard of but which no kitchen in the north could afford to use. I never wasted a scrap and, when my boss wasn't looking, I would scrape up the tiniest crumbs to taste – I could not bear to see them being washed away into the London sewers!

Chocolate was my new medium and I threw myself into the skills of tempering, blending, mixing, and decorating, using every patisserie skill I knew and transposing it into chocolate. I was always eating chocolate, working with chocolate, and seeking out new chocolate shops, especially in Paris. I have had a special relationship with Paris ever since I went there on a school trip, aged 14. I was interested only in the boulangeries, patisseries, and chocolateries that we passed. I still visit Paris every January just after New Year to grab the last festive edge and creativity of the Parisian chocolatiers and patissiers – no macaron is finer than Pierre Hermé's sea-salted caramel macaron, and Patrick Roger's chocolate window display is always stunning.

My dream was to open a stylish chocolaterie where I could sell my own fresh, handmade chocolates and serve the customers myself. After years of searching, one cold, crisp November day I finally found the perfect shop in the perfect location – Camden Passage, famous for its antiques and *objets d'art* shops, in Islington. We opened six months later, in 2006, and I have never looked back.

To me, producing chocolates that are fresh and created by hand using natural ingredients is of paramount importance. Rather than extend the shelf life of my chocolates by including excessive amounts of artificial preservatives, flavors and stabilizers (not to mention refined sugars and inappropriate fats, be they animal, vegetable, or hydrogenated), I use only natural spices, herbs, fruits, and other ingredients, and everything is seasonal. My mission is to create chocolates that are made daily by hand and designed to be eaten on the same day or as soon as possible. The happy result is that in my two shops (I opened another in the City in 2007) we experiment with different flavors, textures, and varieties almost every day; our customers can visit us once, twice, or many times in the same week and there will always be a new chocolate to experience.

I spend a lot of creative time inventing new flavors, textures, and finishes – this is the fun part for anyone making chocolates, whether as a profession or as a hobby, and I love producing tongue-challenging taste combinations. I probably have the invention of my Marmite ganache to thank for my nickname "the Heston Blumenthal of chocolate." But such unusual flavor pairings aren't based on a whim; some can take months to get right.

You might think that tasting the same food over and over every day becomes boring after a while. Not when it comes to chocolate, not for me anyway. I eat – and taste – chocolate every day of every week: first thing in the morning when my palate has not yet been tainted by my mug of rooibos tea or my bowl of oatmeal. This is when I can detect the complexities of the cocoa bean, the hidden notes and characteristics of that particular bean variety. I can taste the same chocolate each day and discover something new about it every time. It is quite amazing and inspiring how from such a humble brown roasted bean can come such an intoxicating and complex experience.

Writing this book, I set out to take you on a journey of chocolate exploration, in which you will learn to really taste – and love – chocolate in all its wonderful forms. You will hopefully learn how to make the perfect truffle, and learn to enjoy my experimental flavor combinations as well as come up with some of your own. If you never get beyond the first chapter, entitled "Unadulterated," which includes my own chocolatey versions of classics such as Christmas pudding and trifle, I will not be heartbroken, but if you grow to love making the green garlic truffles and other more daring recipes in the last chapter, called "Alchemy," you can rest assured that I will be very proud of you! Most importantly, however, I hope that this book will encourage you to become a genuine chocolate aficionado.

But just remember, there are times when eating chocolate has nothing at all to do with skill or identifying flavors, but is simply for pure indulgence. For me, this might mean a sea-salted caramel at coffee break, a Madagascan truffle at 2 o'clock to pick me up, and a dense nugget of my famous chocolate brownie at 4 o'clock – which, for me, is by law teatime, when eating something sweet and indulgent is absolutely compulsory.

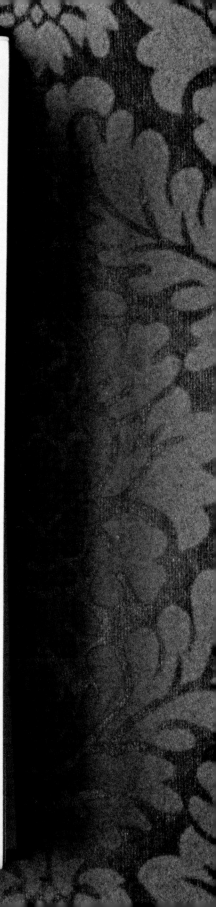

# The first thing you do with chocolate is eat it

The world of chocolate that once seemed so simple ("shall I buy white, milk or dark?") is far more complex – but also ten times more fascinating – than it used to be. Nowadays there are so many different styles, finishes, textures and flavor combinations to choose from that it is easy to feel daunted – and that's before you've even tried to work out what the chocolate tastes of. In the next few pages my aim is to give you all the essential information you need to decide what to buy in the shops, and to also help you through the tasting process.

# Buying the right chocolate

**When choosing which chocolate to buy, people seem to be influenced more by the percentage of cocoa solids than anything else. However, taken on its own this information is not an indicator of quality. In all the recipes in this book, I suggest using a chocolate of a particular origin combined with a certain percentage of cocoa solids. For me, the main reason that Venezuelan chocolate with 72% cocoa solids is different from one with 70% cocoa solids is that the blend of cocoa beans is not the same.**

There are some fantastic manufacturers of chocolate whose products are blissfully easy to get hold of in this age of the internet (see the Suppliers list at the back of this book). You won't be surprised to know that I have some favorite brands, which include Valrhona, Michel Cluizel and Pralus, all from France, and Amedei from Italy. All these brands have their own websites, a look at which will certainly get your juices flowing. Their chocolates have wonderful names, such as Amedei's Toscano Black (a blend) or Valrhona's Manjari from Madagascar. The secret is not to buy too much at a time until you are confident in your choices.

For me, the brand of chocolate is of huge importance, and I hope that my book inspires you to be more adventurous with what you buy, and now and again to splash out on some really high-quality chocolate. However, there will be times when this just isn't practical, and you will wish to buy another variety more commonly found in the supermarket, such as Green & Black's and Lindt. I implore you not to use cheap milk chocolate as the recipes in this book simply won't work if you do. There are lots of recipes where I specify a 70% dark chocolate, for which you can simply use your preferred brand.

I use a special kind of cooking chocolate called couverture for everything I make as it has a higher percentage of cocoa butter, which gives a glossy sheen and clean snap to the finished chocolate. Designed for professional chefs, couverture comes in many forms, from drop-sized pieces to 11-pound bars. But for home cooks standard chocolate works well.

My advice is always buy the best that you can afford and be sympathetic to your ingredients. For example, if you are making a delicate lemon thyme ganache, buy a delicate dark chocolate with 63 to 66% cacao solids, as a chocolate of 85% or above will drown out the fragrant flavors.

*The first thing you do with chocolate...*

# How to taste chocolate

The pleasure of eating chocolate is, of course, the reason for creating your very own handmade chocolates, but there is a particular way to eat chocolate that will really enable you to experience its complex flavors and textures.

We are all guilty of eating chocolate too quickly and eating it before we have time truly to enjoy everything it has to offer. For me, tasting chocolate involves both the mind and the senses, and in particular my sense of smell. So before I eat anything, I smell it first, even if for just a microsecond while it passes beneath my nostrils. Without smelling the ingredients to be used in a new chocolate, I would have no idea of the complexities and interesting flavors to come. Luckily for me,

smell is my most prominent memory trigger, which I use with a vengeance when experimenting with flavor pairings.

There are up to, and possibly more than, 400 flavors and tastes in each piece of fine dark chocolate. It takes time to identify many of the complexities of top-quality chocolate. Of course each piece of chocolate has its own characteristics, but you should always find something in it that sparkles.

If you follow my definitive tasting method below, I guarantee that your relationship with chocolate will never be the same again – and that it will be a long and fulfilling friendship. It is not without reason that the Aztecs referred to chocolate as "the food of the gods."

*1* Look at the chocolate for its color and appearance. A good-quality chocolate will have reddish-brown or deep-brown tones but never black – this is a sign of over-roasted cocoa beans.

*2* Smell the chocolate, breathing deeply, searching for intoxicating, fragrant aromas.

*3* Break the chocolate and listen for a clean snap. If the chocolate has no clean snap then it may have a high amount of vegetable fat or have been poorly tempered (tempering is the technique of heating chocolate in such a way as to ensure a glossy finish and that characteristic snap).

*4* Place a piece of chocolate on your tongue and allow it to melt for the first taste. Chocolate is the only food in the world that melts at exactly body temperature, so be patient and enjoy the experience.

*5* Use the tongue to coat the mouth fully when the chocolate has melted. Breathe deeply through the nose while tasting – this will help the flavors develop and allow you to taste everything the chocolate can offer.

*6* Swallow and experience the aftertaste, if any – an aftertaste can change your view as to whether you like the

chocolate or not. This is very personal, but if the chocolate has a burnt aftertaste then it is usually a sign of poor-quality cocoa beans that have been over-roasted to increase their flavor.

*7* Now take another piece of chocolate and munch or chew this time, as this will release other individual aromas and flavors.

*8* While relaxed, begin to identify the characteristics and complexities of the chocolate, seeking out all it has to offer your palate. You may experience flavors such as toffee, butterscotch, caramel, licorice, coffee, fermented notes, bread crust, salt, and even cheese flavors. All of these may be identified with good-quality chocolate.

*9* Cleanse the palate between different chocolates either by eating dry crackers or bread or by swilling with water.

*10* If tasting with a new ingredient, allow the chocolate to melt fully, then introduce the new ingredient, blending together in the mouth.

The more you taste, the more your confidence will grow, and your tasting palate will improve in a remarkably short space of time – allowing you to identify different varieties of cocoa bean and their flavor characteristics.

# Identifying different chocolates

The taste of chocolate is determined by all sorts of factors: in particular the variety and origin of the cocoa beans, but also how the producer has treated the beans in the fermentation process, and the soil and climatic conditions in any given year. For example, you can detect wet, earthy and woody notes in chocolate made from beans grown in wet and humid areas, while drier areas produce a more acidic and vibrant flavor. This chart is designed to help the tasting process, and should be useful when deciding which chocolate to buy.

| Cocoa bean variety | Origin | Description |
|---|---|---|
| Criollo | Java<br>Madagascar<br>Venezuela | The Criollo is the flawless diamond of all the cocoa bean varieties. It is delicate, complex and highly prized, particularly the rare Porcelana strain. The bean is grown on only a few plantations and is also very susceptible to disease, so makes up just 5 to 10 per cent of the world's production. Producers such as Amedei and Domori (both in Italy), Pierre Marcolini (in Belgium), and Scharffen Berger (in California) all make small quantities of chocolate using Criollo beans, which is extremely expensive. Venezuelan Criollo beans are known for their delicate floral aromas, while the Madagascan variety has greater acidity. Those from Java have a more robust cocoa flavor and are often used in milk chocolate to give balance and character. |
| Trinitario | Grenada<br>Haiti<br>Jamaica<br>Trinidad<br>Venezuela | The Trinitario variety is originally from Trinidad in the Caribbean, where the Spanish first cultivated it in the 17th century. With its fine, delicate character but robust finish, this variety sits between the Criollo and Forastero beans in terms of flavor. The Trinitario is generally used for blending by bigger producers, although Valrhona and some others make an exquisitely fragranced chocolate from single-estate Trinitario varieties, which matches perfectly with florals and delicate fruits. The Jamaican Trinitario, on the other hand, can release rum, juniper, and even woody notes of cedar. |
| Forastero | Côte d'Ivoire<br>Ghana<br>São Tomé | Bold, strong, and full of character, the Forastero bean is often blended with other varieties to add strength. It is the world's most widespread cocoa bean, cultivated largely for mass production. Generally, the bitterness in this variety is low, while the chocolatey taste that we all love is high. The bean grown in Ghana has coffee and tobacco flavors, while notes of red fruits, cinnamon and vanilla can all be present in Forastero beans from São Tomé; the variety from the Côte d'Ivoire has tobacco and leathery notes. |

The thing that all cocoa-producing countries (there are, of course, others besides those mentioned in the chart overleaf) have in common is that they are within twenty degrees either side of the Equator. Very little chocolate is actually manufactured in the tropics, most of the best-quality chocolate that you buy being made in the US or Europe. The magic of chocolate is that the variety of flavors is infinite, based on the unlimited scope to blend different cocoa beans – whether different varieties or even the same variety from different countries.

Customers come into my shop and say to me "I love Madagascan chocolate" or "I love Venezuelan chocolate." I adore the fact that people care so much about the provenance of their chocolate, but this idea is not as simple as it sounds. Two manufacturers sourcing their raw materials in one country can produce chocolate from the same variety of cocoa bean, yet one can be terrible because the beans have been poorly cultivated and processed, and the other may be the world's best as the cultivators grow fantastic beans and know how to process them. Bear this in mind when you go shopping.

Given the abundance of flavors and tastes present in a piece of fine chocolate, it is no surprise that identifying its particular characteristics can be a challenge – though an enjoyable one at that. The section below will introduce you to some of the key characteristics of chocolates originating from certain countries, but bear in mind my warning that flavors can vary enormously even between chocolates made from beans grown in the same region. I also give some ideas for different uses and possible pairings with different ingredients. More detailed notes on how to pair specific ingredients with certain chocolates are given on page 29.

## Africa

**Madagascar**: Fruity, slightly acidic and feels light in the mouth; ideal for summer and tangy flavors. There is sometimes a hint of an alcoholic flavor that stems from the fermentation of the cocoa beans. I love using Madagascan chocolate for my dark chocolate truffles and it also goes well with summer berries; try it in a chocolate and raspberry tart, or in a sauce for summer fruits or a fruit ice cream.

**Ghana**: Bold and robust, not too bitter, and with a definite tobacco and coffee edge. This is a fantastic baking variety as it has a strong chocolate taste with a hit of cocoa at the end. Try using it in brownies and coffee or chocolate desserts. It also

makes a wonderful strong and robust dark chocolate truffle. If you fancy trying something more adventurous, Ghanaian dark chocolate has enough strength and character to work really well in savory recipes.

## South America

**Venezuela**: Criollo varieties have a delicate and fragrant finish, especially those of Chuao and Porcelana strains, and are often unusual and highly complex. In general, Venezuelan varieties are fragrant and not overpowering, even with a high percentage of cocoa solids. The flavors tend to be earthy, with hints of toasted bread crust, spices and even tobacco. I use Venezuelan chocolate to make a really indulgent hot chocolate. It also goes well with nuts and spices such as cloves and mild chile, as well as woody herbs.

**Ecuador**: A new favorite of mine, with unique characteristics including banana, blackberry, hazelnuts and citrus fruits. A delicate fragrance appears during eating and permeates through to the nose, and an earthy finish rounds off the chocolate. Hints of coffee, vanilla, and delicate spices are also present. Ecuadorean chocolate makes a wonderful mousse or soufflé, and works well with gentle spices and tropical fruits.

## Caribbean

**Dominican Republic**: Strong robust flavors, often with hints of licorice, treacle toffee and molasses. It gives an intense, long finish and a clear cocoa taste in the mouth. Think autumn and winter – rich caramel, sticky toffee pudding, hot chocolate sauces, chocolate puddings, and strong hot chocolate. Warm winter spices all work well.

**Grenada**: Small producers growing rare and interesting varieties are coming up with increasingly complex flavors from floral and woody to acidic and fruity. Hunt out the Grenada Chocolate Company bar (see Suppliers list at the back of the book), which is outstanding. Eat this chocolate on its own to fully appreciate the complex and intriguing flavors. There is no need to blend or mix it with anything.

**Trinidad**: Delicate character, woody and spicy, with chocolate, grassy and green tastes; notes of citrus and tropical fruits are often present. It works beautifully in baked pastries and biscuits, and combines well with honey, figs, and oranges.

### Indonesia

**Java**: In my view, cocoa beans from Java make incredible milk chocolate, with 35 to 40% cocoa solids. It is wonderfully creamy (milk being predominant), with a sweet, sometimes caramel or toffee, finish. It is not complex in terms of cocoa flavor, but is comforting and indulgent. Some milk chocolate contains malt extract, which gives a rounded and warm taste. Cinnamon, nutmeg and other winter spices work well with milk chocolate, while adding roasted almonds and hazelnuts makes for a classic combination.

The intense sugars of naturally dried fruits also combine well with milk chocolate.

### Other chocolate products

**Cacao nibs**: These intense and aromatic crunchy nuggets of cacao (pictured top right) are what you get once the cacao beans have been roasted and cracked: it is these that are then ground up into chocolate liquor from which chocolate is made. You can sprinkle them on your granola or oatmeal, and use them in cookies and desserts. They are fantastic used to make a warm cacao-nib tea, too, and even better on ice cream. I use them in several recipes in this book, including the cacao-nib cookies on page 36 and the muscovado chocolate cakes on page 82.

**Cocoa powder**: This is produced by the removal of most of the cocoa butter from the chocolate liquor, using a press. In its untreated state, natural cocoa powder has a reddish color and a relatively low pH level, causing a sour or acidic taste. I prefer top-quality alkalized or Dutch-processed cacao, the kind made by the top chocolate manufacturers, which has a milder flavor and is reddish-brown in color. Don't confuse it with hot cocoa mix, which is sweetened and flavored and only meant for making beverages. It may cost more, but since the flavor is so good you don't need to use so much of it.

**White chocolate**: Is this really chocolate? Well, the argument goes on, as white chocolate contains zero percent cocoa solids. My view is that as long as the white chocolate is made with 100% cocoa butter and not vegetable fat, then it does count as chocolate. The other components are sugar, milk powder, vanilla and sometimes soy lecithin. Just one word of warning: white chocolate is the most sensitive to overheating, so always melt it very slowly and gently.

# How to make a chocolate truffle

There is nothing quite like a smooth, silky and creamy truffle – crisp chocolate breaking into a melting middle, revealing different flavors, infusions and textures within. Over the next few pages I'm going to explain how to make a simple chocolate truffle. Once you have mastered the process, you will be able to make any of the truffles in this book. I think you'll be surprised how easy it can be, and you don't need go out and buy lots of expensive equipment.

The two key elements of a truffle are the ganache – an emulsion of melted chocolate and cream (or other liquid) – and the tempered chocolate, which is used for coating the truffle. Both techniques are invaluable for many of the recipes in this book, and not just for the truffles.

# The ganache

There is a language particular to chocolate-making, and ganache is one word you will hear me use a lot throughout this book. Ganache is, technically speaking, an emulsion of melted chocolate and cream – though many liquids other than cream are also used these days. The creamy-chocolate combination is believed to have derived from a mistake in a chocolate kitchen – some say in France, others Switzerland – in the 19th century, when an apprentice spilled cream into melting chocolate. The head chocolatier is reputed to have shouted "Ganache!" to the apprentice, presumably in rebuke, though the novice turned out to be not such a fool after all.

Ganache can be used to make truffles, of course, but you will discover that it has all sorts of other uses. For example, you can pour a drizzle of warm ganache over fresh berries and fruits, or pour it generously over ice cream. Or try spreading it over a cake: my garden mint ganache on page 96 works wonderfully in this way. Some of my more unusual, savory ganaches can be used as sauces to accompany meat and fish, while others (such as the salt and pepper ganache on page 84) are stunning used as a dipping sauce.

In this book I will introduce you to all manner of weird and wonderful ganaches that I use to fill my truffles. As you will discover, I get extremely excited about the fillings as they are the truffle's hidden secret that delivers the provocative and intoxicating flavors. Over the past ten years there has been a revolution in chocolate fillings, with all sorts of exotic and innovative ingredients now being used. In the 1980s, you would find lots of rose creams, hard toffee and lots and lots of fondant centers. Thankfully, we have become much more experimental in our tastes, as have patissiers and chocolatiers, who seek inspiration from all corners of the globe. It is now commonplace to find lemongrass, pink peppercorns, jasmine tea and sea salt in chocolate. You will find much more about my ideas on combining chocolate with other flavors on page 29.

First of all, you need to decide which type and variety of chocolate to use. In the introduction we looked at types and varieties of chocolate from different bean varieties, so use this as a guide if you want to try some out. I nearly always choose Madagascan for my dark chocolate truffles as I like the balance of fruitiness with the robust cocoa flavors. Taste your chocolate, closing your eyes to experience all its hidden depths and undernotes of flavors and aromas. This will help you later when you are testing your ganache.

A ganache can be used to make truffles in two different ways: it can be either chilled and then hand rolled, or piped while still soft into a chocolate shell. The first method is the more traditional and also the easier. You will discover in the book that ganaches are by no means uniform in texture: some can be used for rolling or piping, while others have a lighter and softer texture when set and are suitable only for being piped into shells.

For beginners setting out on their truffle-making journey, the perfect starting-point is the classic hand-rolled chocolate truffle, with a creamy ganache center coated with a crispy dark chocolate shell and dusted in cocoa.

# How to make a classic ganache

For a classic dark chocolate ganache, use the following recipe as your base. The quantities given should produce up to 50 chocolates.

**9 ounces dark chocolate**

**1 cup plus 2 tablespoons heavy cream**

**½ cup packed light brown sugar**

First, chop the chocolate into small, even-sized pieces or use the small chocolate disks called pistoles, which require no chopping, and place in a heat proof mixing bowl. Place the cream and sugar in a small saucepan. Bring to a boil and simmer for 1 minute. This will fully dissolve the sugar and kill any bacteria that may be present in the cream.

Turn off the heat and allow the cream to cool for 1 minute. (Pouring the cream onto the chocolate while boiling will scorch it and cause the cocoa butter in the chocolate to separate, resulting in a curdled ganache.) Now pour the rested cream over the chocolate pieces and mix well with a rubber spatula or whisk until smooth and very glossy.

Allow the ganache to cool to room temperature. Place it, covered, in the fridge for at least 2 hours or until fully set.

## Rolling the truffles

Remove the set ganache from the fridge. Using a teaspoon, scoop even-sized pieces of the chocolate and place onto a sheet of parchment paper.

Powder your hands with cocoa powder, and then, using your fingers, begin to roll the ganache into evenly shaped spheres. Take care not to take too long over this as the ganache will begin to melt and become impossible to roll. Place the rolled truffles back onto the parchment paper.

You can eat the truffles at this point, as they are dusted in cocoa powder, but I think a real truffle needs to have a crisp shell to protect it and to give a textural difference. To create this shell, you will need to coat your truffle in tempered chocolate. (If you are not eating the dusted truffles, place them in the fridge until needed.)

# Tempering chocolate

**This is the most important skill to learn when you are making truffles, and is also essential for making chocolate bars and molded shapes. Tempered chocolate is used to create a shell around the rolled ganache, and can also be used for decorating truffles (see page 26).**

If you have ever melted chocolate, you may have noticed that when it cools and becomes solid it is no longer hard but often soft, crumbly, separated, dull in appearance and less pleasant to eat. Tempering is the process that gives a crisp, shiny and smooth texture to chocolate once it has been melted. Without getting too scientific, it is useful to know that when liquid chocolate cools and re-solidifies, the fats in the cocoa butter start to crystallize. If this occurs in an uncontrolled fashion, a jumble of crystals of varying size and type form, causing the surface of the chocolate to appear mottled, streaky and dull, and making the chocolate crumble rather than snap when broken. The point of tempering is to control the crystallization of the molecules in the chocolate so that only one particular type of crystal is present.

Tempering can seem complicated, but I will show you two of the most effective ways of doing it: the "seeding" method and the "marble-slab" method. Master just one of the methods and there will be no stopping your creative urges!

## The seeding method

I recommend that you try this method first as it requires no special equipment and it's also very clean – no pouring chocolate onto your worktop involved! All you need is a glass or stainless-steel mixing bowl that fits over a saucepan, to melt your chocolate in. A digital thermometer is helpful but not essential – in fact I prefer to test the temperature of the chocolate by more simple means.

Begin by chopping 1¼ pounds of dark chocolate into small, even-sized pieces or use pistoles, small chocolate disks that require no chopping. Place two-thirds of the chocolate in a heatproof mixing bowl.

Fill a saucepan with enough water to reach just below the bowl when placed on top of the pan. Place over medium heat and allow the water to get hot. Place the bowl over the water and let it melt extremely slowly for at least 1 hour. The idea is to keep the chocolate just at its melting temperature. The chocolate won't go over this temperature if the water isn't simmering or boiling, just hot. This will ensure that all the fats, sugars and crystals have melted evenly. If the water boils it can burn the chocolate, which will then become grainy and unusable, so take care.

Once the chocolate has fully melted, remove the bowl from the saucepan and place on a towel or cloth. Now, while mixing vigorously, add the remaining chocolate pieces all in one go. Keep mixing until the pieces are fully melted and the chocolate cools to 80–82°F – this is when the chocolate begins to crystallize and harden. If you don't have a digital thermometer, you can check the temperature by dipping an icing spatula into the chocolate and then touching your bottom lip. The chocolate should feel neither cold nor warm, but at body temperature. With a little practice you will soon feel confident using this simple method – it is the way I prefer to do it.

Now place the bowl back over the water until the temperature has reached 88–89°F. This is known as the working temperature, and means that your chocolate has been tempered and is ready to use. To test this manually, dip the end of a knife or spatula into the chocolate and allow to set (see right). If the chocolate is smooth, glossy and brittle when set, then you have successfully tempered it.

*Seeding - a definition*

The term "seeding" – used in chemistry to describe the addition of small crystals to a liquid to induce crystallization – is used because small pieces of solid chocolate are stirred slowly into melted chocolate to incorporate the liquid chocolate with crystals. Maintaining the correct temperature is crucial to the process.

## The marble slab method

Marble-slab tempering can seem a daunting prospect to the uninitiated, but like anything it just takes a bit of practice. The marble-slab method achieves good results more consistently than the seeding method, especially for larger amounts of chocolate, so it's a technique worth cracking.

The reason for using marble or granite is that both have remarkable cooling qualities, even in a warm kitchen. The cooling surface builds the hardening crystals in the chocolate to give a beautiful shine and crisp texture to your chocolates.

If you have a marble or granite worktop, you can obviously use that. Don't be frightened about pouring molten chocolate onto your worktop – I promise that the chocolate won't end up on the floor! Alternatively, my top tip for buying a marble slab is to visit your local building supplier or tile outlet. Be bold and ask for a broken, disused or unwanted piece of marble or granite, as you will be surprised to find that you might even get a freebie, especially if you offer some of your handmade chocolates in return! The minimum size to temper 2 pounds of chocolate is about 24 x 36 inches. The only other bit of equipment you will need is a triangular cake decorating comb though you can also use two metal icing spatulas.

Over hot water, melt at least 2 pounds of chocolate to a maximum temperature of 131°F. Do not let the water boil or simmer but keep it hot and allow the chocolate to melt for at least 2 hours. This will ensure that all the fats, sugars and crystals have melted evenly.

Pour two-thirds of the chocolate onto a granite or marble surface, leaving the remainder over hot water to maintain its temperature. Spread the chocolate evenly over the slab with an icing spatula and then scrape it back on itself with another spatula. Repeat this action until the chocolate cools to 80–82°F, which is when the chocolate begins to crystallize and harden. You can check this temperature by using a digital thermometer or by touching some chocolate, with the icing spatula, onto your bottom lip: the chocolate should feel at body temperature.

Now scrape the cool chocolate into the remaining warm chocolate (still at 131°F) and mix very well until fully incorporated: be vigorous and confident, and work the chocolate smoothly. The mixing is very important at this stage as you need to make the temperature even throughout the chocolate. The temperature should now be 88–89°F, the so-called working temperature. As with the seeding method, to check if the chocolate is tempered, dip the end of the icing spatula into the chocolate and place it aside to set. If the chocolate sets with a shine and is crisp, then you have tempered your chocolate perfectly.

Once you have your bowl of tempered chocolate, it is ready to use. As the chocolate will cool down, you may need to maintain the working temperature; to do this simply warm the chocolate over hot water for 30 seconds or so.

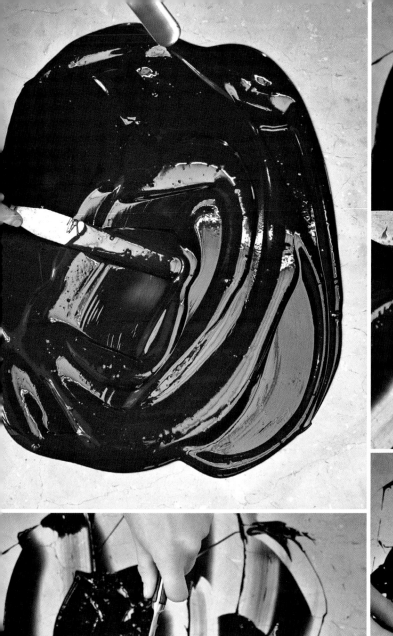

## Tempering tips

If you are tempering small amounts of chocolate, it is best to use the seeding method, as tempering less than 2 pounds on a marble slab is very difficult (even for me!). This is another reason that the seeding method is the better one to start off with, so you don't waste too much chocolate if it all goes horribly wrong. The minimum amount of chocolate you can easily temper at a time is 12 ounces.

If, after the tempering process, the chocolate on the spatula is streaky, grainy or dull, there are ways you can try to fix it:
- You may need simply to continue your mixing to emulsify the chocolate fully.
- The temperature of the chocolate may still be too high and you may need to temper it again briefly on the marble slab. If you are using the seeding method, add a little more chocolate and keep mixing until the chocolate has cooled and is smooth.
- You may not have melted your chocolate sufficiently at the beginning, in which case it will need to be returned to the heat and allowed to come to the correct melted temperature, at which point you can start the tempering process again.

Any unused tempered chocolate can be left to set at room temperature, stored in a cool dry place, and re-melted for your next batch of chocolates. It can be re-melted three or four times.

## Coating the truffles in tempered chocolate

**The next step is to coat your hand-rolled truffles in tempered chocolate. Be prepared to get messy, but you'll need to resist licking your fingers until all your truffles have been coated.**

First, remove the rolled truffles from the fridge and set them aside for 5 minutes to remove the chill. Then take a truffle in your left hand and dip the fingers of your right hand into the tempered chocolate. Place the truffle into the chocolate on your right hand, dip your left hand into the chocolate and begin to roll the truffle gently in your fingers, evenly coating the truffle. Take care to cover all areas, leaving no holes.

Once it is covered in tempered chocolate, immediately place the truffle in a deep bowl of cocoa powder so that it becomes fully coated – rolling or burying the truffle or simply shaking the bowl around should do the trick. Allow the coated truffles to set completely. Remove from the cocoa powder and place on a plate or in a bowl ready to be eaten, or tuck them into a gift box if they are to be a present.

## Tempering chart

| Chocolate | Melting temp. | Crystallizing temp. | Working temp. |
|---|---|---|---|
| Dark | 131°F | 80–82°F | 88–89°F |
| Milk | 122–131°F | 79–80°F | 84–86°F |
| White | 122°F | 79–80°F | 84–86°F |

# *M*olding chocolate

**Once you feel confident with tempering you can experiment with molding chocolate into shells, bars and shapes.**

## Using chocolate shells

The job of filling chocolate shells is admittedly more difficult than hand rolling and coating, but the results can be fantastic. In this book I have included several recipes for ganaches that are designed solely to be piped into hollow chocolate shells; they are softer than the ganaches use for rolling. Note, however, that some ganaches work equally well whether hand rolled or piped into chocolate shells – it's just a matter of either chilling the ganache or using it while warm.

I make my own chocolate shells – using tempered chocolate and a special chocolate mold – but you can easily buy them ready-made online (see the Suppliers list at the back of the book). They are usually labelled as 'truffle spheres' or "truffle shells." Some supermarkets now stock chocolate *petit four* shells or cups, which can also be used.

### How to fill chocolate shells

Once the ganache you have made has been cooling at room temperature for 30 minutes, it should be flowing but not too warm. You can check the temperature by dipping an icing spatula into the chocolate and touching your bottom lip with it. If it feels hot, then allow the ganache to cool more; if it feels tepid but not cold, you are ready to go.

Use a piping bag to fill the shells (still upright in their packing tray), taking care to leave a $1/8$ inch gap at the top to allow you to seal the chocolate once the ganache has set. Place the filled shells aside and let set overnight or for at least 6 hours.

Once the ganache has set, it's time either to cap off the filled shells or to coat the whole thing (in the case of spherical shells only), using tempered chocolate; the main object is to seal out the air so that the ganache is preserved for longer. Both processes become much easier with practice.

To cap off the filled shells, spoon a little tempered chocolate onto the top of each, then, using an icing spatula or scraper, remove any excess – effectively sealing the top of the shell with chocolate. Allow to set for at least 20 minutes.

To coat the shells rather than sealing them, simply take the tempered chocolate in both hands and roll the filled shell around in your fingertips until the entire truffle is coated. Now place the coated chocolate (hole side down) onto silicone paper and leave to set for 20 minutes.

## Making chocolate bars and shapes

Once you feel confident with the tempering process, it is easy to make your own chocolate bars. The recipes for bars in this book are a good starting-point and will hopefully inspire you to go off and create your own. All you need is a mold of some sort. There is a vast array on the market, from professional molds to easy-to-use molds aimed at home cooks (see the Suppliers list). Prepare your chocolate molds before use by polishing them with pure, unbleached cotton wool to remove any finger marks, grease, and dust.

Spoon or pour the tempered chocolate into the mold, then gently tap or shake it to release any air bubbles that may be trapped in the chocolate. Place the chocolate in the fridge for a maximum of 15 minutes, after which time the chocolate should be set. Invert the mold onto a clean kitchen towel so that the chocolate doesn't break.

Another method for creating chocolate shapes uses ganache rather than tempered chocolate, as in my recipe on page 17. Simply pour the ganache into a baking tray, leave to cool, then refrigerate. Once the chocolate has set, you can cut it into shapes. This can be done with any of the thicker ganaches designed to be hand rolled into truffles.

## Looking after your chocolates

I hope that you will find the chocolates so irresistible that they won't last more than a few hours. Nevertheless, it's important that you know **not to store your homemade chocolates in the fridge**. If chocolates become too cold, when they come into contact with the warm air condensation immediately appears and causes the sugars to be extracted from the chocolate, resulting in what's known as a "sugar bloom." The chocolate becomes wet and sticky and, eventually, very dull and unappealing. Furthermore, the flavors will not be as prominent and aromatic.

The only exception to this rule are truffles that are simply rolled ganache dusted in cocoa powder, i.e. without a tempered-chocolate coating. I store these in the fridge as I would ganache, in an airtight container.

To store your other chocolates properly, put them on (or wrap them in) parchment paper and then in an airtight container. Place them in a cool, dark place away from heat and strong odors. Allow any chocolate to come to room temperature before eating.

The temperatures in people's homes can vary, and different ingredients have naturally different preserving times, but as a general rule truffles and ganaches should be consumed within seven days. If alcohol is added, you can increase the shelf life to three weeks, though you need to make sure that you don't boil off all the alcohol when making the ganache. That is one reason why alcoholic chocolates make great gifts, particularly at Christmas.

If your chocolates are a gift, wrap them in cellophane or colored foil, or arrange them in a chocolate box, then give them to the recipient as soon as possible. Write the enjoy-by date on a label or on the bottom of the box. Chocolate bars are particularly good as presents because these can last for up to one year. If you add dried fruit or nuts, however, reduce that time to around three months.

Never throw away any left-over ganache; save it to pour over ice cream or fruit or whatever you fancy. It can be stored in the fridge for one week if water- or cream-based, or for two weeks if alcohol- or caramel-based. Any ganache can be frozen for up to three months in an airtight container. Simply place it in the fridge to defrost slowly for six hours or so. You can then either roll it as it is, or, if you are piping it or using it as a sauce, warm it gently in a water bath, stirring well.

# Taking it further

**If you master the basic truffle recipe, you'll be doing well. For those of you inspired to take the whole process further, here are some ideas for decorating the truffles, for matching flavors to chocolates, and for making different kinds of ganache. Of course, the flavor-matching tips and alternative ganaches can be used for all sorts of chocolate recipes, not just those for truffles.**

If you need inspiration beyond the ideas in this book, why not go to your nearest chocolate shop and have a look, and even buy a selection of just four to six truffles to try. Be brave and show your enthusiasm in the chocolate shop and ask if you can taste one or two. A good chocolatier may allow you to taste his signature chocolate or the day's special creation.

## Decorating truffles

If the simple cocoa-dusted look described above (see page 22) isn't for you, then you can decorate the truffles instead. Below is a selection of classic and contemporary ways to make your truffles look extra special with piped chocolate, powders and even gold or silver leaf.

A simple way to decorate is just to roll the truffles in a ground spice, herb or other ingredient to add a particular flavor, texture or look. You can do this either before coating the truffle in tempered chocolate or afterwards (before the chocolate has set) – the latter gives a more instant hit of flavor or texture. Alternatively, you can simply mix the ingredient into the tempered chocolate and then apply as normal. Throughout the book you will find all sorts of ideas as to ingredients to use, but here are some favorites of mine: pink peppercorns, ground spices, ground coffee beans, sesame seeds, desiccated coconut, chopped nuts, and dried and crystallized flowers such as lavender, rose and violet. I also like making my own powders that can be used in the same way; see opposite for a couple of recipes.

When applying the following types of decoration, you must coat the truffles first with tempered chocolate and leave them to set.

You can pipe tempered chocolate onto truffles in all sorts of clever ways. All you need is a small piping bag, which you can either buy ready-made or make out of parchment paper. Fill the bag two-thirds full with tempered chocolate and fold the open end down firmly to seal in the chocolate. If you have made your own, snip off the tip to form a small hole – the finer the hole, the more professional your finished chocolates will look. If you have a ready-made bag, choose a small nozzle.

Firmly squeeze the piping bag from the top and allow the chocolate to fall on top of the truffles, moving with a swift and even movement; it is important to avoid letting the bag come into contact with the truffle. The secret to piping is to practice on parchment paper beforehand. In no time you will be piping beautiful swirls, filigree and lattice patterns, polka dots and even lettering for personalized truffles.

To decorate your truffles with gold or silver leaf, or other decorative edibles, simply pipe a very small dot of tempered chocolate onto the truffle and apply the decoration with steady hands.

# Homemade powders

While it is nice to splash out on some gold leaf now and again, there are all sorts of powders that you can make at home to use for decorating truffles.

### Keffir Lime-leaf powder

For this recipe you will need 12 fresh lime leaves (with the central vein removed) and Keffir sugar. In batches, process the leaves and sugar in a coffee grinder or blender to break them down. Transfer to a heavy mortar and pestle to grind to a fine powder. Pass it through a sieve to remove any stalks. The process requires a certain amount of elbow grease and a good deal of patience, but I promise you it's worth it. Sprinkle the powder onto parchment paper and leave to dry for 12 hours. The same method can be used to create powders using herb leaves such as curry and bay.

### Tea powders

These powders are very simple to make and can be used to coat ganache or to add special flavor to chocolate bars. Buy the finest tea leaves you can possibly afford, as quality means flavor and purity; for an intense flavor look for fragranced tea, such as Earl Grey, Lapsang Souchong, or fruit-infused tea. Spread the tea onto parchment paper for 1 hour to dry out slightly. Grind with a mortar and pestle until very fine, then pass through a fine strainer. To use, roll the ganache in the powder either before coating in tempered chocolate or afterwards.

Stored in an airtight container, these powders will keep for a month.

## Combining flavors

You will find plenty of ideas for flavor matches in this book, some more outlandish than others, but to help you to experiment on your own, I have devised a table to suggest ingredients to pair with particular types of chocolate – predominantly dark, of course. It takes time to discover new tongue-dazzling combinations, but don't let that put you off trying! If you need to refresh your memory as to the characteristics of the various chocolates, turn to page 12.

### Madagascan

- Pairs well with summer berries, including raspberries, strawberries and cherries.
- Sea salt enhances the chocolate, adding sparkle and character; combines fantastically with salted caramel.
- Goes well with tangy flavors, including lemongrass, wasabi or horseradish, cranberries, passion fruit, gin and fruity red wine.
- For a more unusual, eye-catching pairing, try combining with hard cheeses or, my favorite, Marmite.

### Venezuelan

- Many types of chocolate work well with nuts and Venezuelan is no exception. Almonds and hazelnuts work particularly well, and so do toasted sesame seeds.
- Woody herbs, such as rosemary, thyme, lavender and sage, are good; basil matches well too.
- Spices such as cinnamon, cardamom, nutmeg, black or Sichuan pepper, mild chile and cloves pair well individually or as mixed flavors.
- Other ingredients to try are dried fruits or, for the more daring among you, geranium and celeriac.

### Dominican Republic

- Spices, such as warming chile, black pepper, coriander, and cinnamon, all work well.
- Brazil nuts and walnuts add bite and balance.
- Apples and pears offer an easy match.

### Trinidad

- Honey, figs, and oranges.
- Green tea or fresh green herbs such as basil and cilantro.
- Cedarwood, sandalwood and pine all match well, as do toasted nuts.

### Ecuadorean

- This chocolate positively sparkles when combined with fresh and dried coconut, or with garden mint.
- Works well with concentrated fruit compotes; marmalades and jams, and all tropical fruits balance well.
- Roasted nuts, coffee and muscovado caramel are easy to match and versatile.
- Gentle spices, such as pink peppercorns, green cardamom, cassia and saffron, are all good.

### Ghanaian

- Try with chile, coffee, or garlic.

### Milk

- Slow-roasted almonds and hazelnuts make for a classic combination; add a touch of sea salt and you have an outstanding blend.
- As a general rule, a touch of sea salt can temper the sweetness and balance the flavors of milk chocolate.
- Cinnamon, nutmeg and other winter spices work well, adding warmth and comfort. Cumin, cardamom and fresh ginger in syrup are good too.
- The intense caramelized sugars of naturally dried fruits such as apricots, peaches, and figs can be stunning with milk chocolate. Citrus fruits also work well.
- For something a bit different, try combining with creamy cheeses or chèvre, and fennel seed.

### White

- A motley array of flavors work well with white chocolate, including pink peppercorns, cumin, nutmeg, lemongrass, goat's cheese, sweet potato and pumpkin. Take your pick!

## Different types of ganache

Traditionally, ganaches are cream-based (see page 17). But these days, chocolatiers like me use all sorts of other liquids. For example, if heavy cream is too rich for your taste buds, then try using light cream, milk, yogurt, cream cheese, goat's milk, or even soy milk. But the liquid can be as simple as pure spring water, fruit juice or alcohol. It's these dairy-free liquids that I'm focusing on here.

Commonly known in the trade as "water ganaches," dairy-free ganaches are in vogue for their super-clean flavors and reduced fat content. Creating them is surprisingly simple and will extend your chocolate repertoire greatly. The method is essentially the same as with cream, but you don't have to boil the liquids as vigorously to kill the bacteria (in order to increase the shelf life). I use many of the liquids described below in the book; here are a few general guidelines:

**Water**: Most simply, you can create a guilt-free truffle by using just water as your liquid. The result can be as smooth, creamy and indulgent as if you were using heavy cream.

**Juices**: You can use all manner of fruit juices, either singly or in combination. Fresh orange juice, for example, makes the most mouth-watering orange ganache. Some reliable combinations include: coconut and pineapple; peach and apricot; and pomegranate, grape and cherry.

You can add a vibrant shot of flavor to any ganache by making your own juices from fresh herbs and spices, using a centrifugal juice extractor. Try combining ginger and lemongrass; green apple and horseradish; or galangal (or fresh ginger) and Thai basil. These juices can be added before cooking, or afterwards for a raw intense flavor.

**Alcohol**: You can use alcoholic liquids such as red, white or dessert wine, Champagne, whisky, Cognac and all manner of liqueurs. When using spirits and liqueurs, you need to add water to dilute the overpowering strength of the alcohol.

**Tea and coffee**: Strong brews of tea work well, and they can be supplemented with pure essential oil (for example bergamot oil for Earl Grey tea) if a burst of extra flavor is needed. And coffee too, of course. Done well, a coffee ganache can be amazing – nothing like the old-fashioned coffee creams of our childhood, which were sugary and lacked depth of flavor.

**Infusions**: A classic way to create complex and innovative flavors in a ganache is by using an infusion. I use the infusion method a lot in this book, both the cold and the hot method. Cold infusion creates a delicate flavor with a fresh, pure and clean taste, while a hot infusion creates a more pungent and stronger flavor. Experimenting is the key, but it's worth noting that hard herbs and florals, such as lavender, rosemary and thyme, and hard spices, such as cinnamon, benefit from being heated to release their essential oils. Soft florals and herbs, such as rose petals and basil, benefit from cold infusion as their delicate flavors would be killed by heating.

To infuse basil using the cold method, for example, tear the basil leaves roughly and place into the cream or water and cover with a piece of parchment paper. Leave for 24 hours in a cool place (but not the fridge). You will need a large quantity of herbs to create a strong flavor using this method.

To infuse lavender and lemon, for example, using the hot method, place the lavender flowers and lemon zest into the liquid and warm to 167°F, then turn off the heat and allow the flavors to infuse until the liquid is cold. Strain out the ingredients and reheat the liquid to create your ganache.

It is not an exact science, but as a rough guide, per water use 1½ soft herbs of ¾–1 sturdy herbs and florals.

## Experimenting with flavors

First of all, take your desired ingredients and "live with them" for a few days. Get to know them well – smell them, taste them, study them. Then it is time to introduce the flavors to each other (if you are creating a blend) and to introduce the flavor (or flavors) to the chocolate.

Taking Marmite as an example, I would begin by smelling the Marmite gently and then with a deep strong sniff. This allows me to identify both the delicate and deeper, hidden aromas. Then I taste, carefully coating every inch of my mouth. I write down all the things I experience – salty, sweet, tangy, yeasty, earthy, etc. – and I then begin to taste my different chocolates. At this point, the balance of flavor is often nowhere near perfect, so the dilution begins, my aim being to achieve a Marmite flavor that is neither overpowering nor too weak.

I then heat my water and Marmite mixture gently in a pan, adding a little brown sugar and then my chocolate, melting it into the liquid until smooth and glossy. The method is that of an apothecary – mixing, blending, swirling and watching wonderful and magical things happen.

# Unadulterated

I am a purist and relish all things natural and unadulterated, so I had to include a chapter to celebrate this. To enjoy chocolate in its purest form, whether sweet or savory, is one of the most intense food experiences you are likely to have. Many of the recipes in this chapter are twists on a traditional classic, but the focus is always on using lots of real cocoa and real chocolate. Unadulterated recipes show off and highlight the complexities and hidden depths of cocoa that are often lost through over-processing and manufacturing. In fact, it may take your taste buds some time to adjust to the stronger flavors and tastes of real chocolate, but I promise that by the end you will be forever entranced by this most mysterious of ingredients.

# Paul's Aztec-style hot chocolate

By adding spices of your choice to this recipe, you can create your own favorite hot chocolate. I took the Aztecs' idea of using only water, not milk or cream, and of cooking the liquid to thicken naturally.

**2 tablespoons light muscovado sugar (more if you like it sweeter)**

**3 tablespoons alkalized cocoa powder**

**3½ ounces Caribbean 66% dark chocolate**

**Ground spice e.g. chile, cinnamon, nutmeg, cardamom, or ginger (optional)**

Heat 1³/4 cups water, the sugar and cocoa powder in a saucepan and simmer for 3 minutes. Chop the chocolate into pieces and add to the pan. Using an electric hand blender, blend for 1 minute, adding any spices that you are using at this point. Bring the hot chocolate back to the simmer for 2 minutes and serve.

**Variation**: For a Mayan hot chocolate, add a pinch of pure ground chile powder, ¹/2 teaspoon of cinnamon and ¹/4 teaspoon of freshly grated nutmeg to the chocolate while it's still in the pan. Mix well and allow to infuse off the heat for 2 minutes before serving.

# Chocolate syrups

An adults-only version of the chocolate syrups we enjoyed on our ice cream as children.

**1 teaspoon fine sea salt**

**2 cups organic sugar**

**10½ ounces 70% dark chocolate, coarsely chopped**

**3 tablespoons golden syrup or light corn syrup**

Bring 1¹/3 cups water, the salt, and sugar to a simmer in a saucepan. Remove from the heat and add the chocolate. Blend well using a hand blender or food processor. Add the golden syrup and blend again. Either use the syrup warm, or allow it to cool and then store in an airtight container or plastic bottle.

## Chocolate syrup variations

**Alcoholic syrup**: Use half the amount of water, then add ¹/2 cup plus 3 tablespoons of your chosen liqueur or spirit after the golden (or corn) syrup.

**Spiced syrup**: Add cinnamon, chile, nutmeg, vanilla, star anise or cloves to the liquid pan and allow to infuse for 30 minutes. Strain any spices out, then reboil before adding the chocolate.

**Herb syrup**: Add chopped herbs such as lavender, rosemary, basil or lemongrass to the simmering water and sugar and allow to infuse off the heat for 30 minutes. Strain off the herbs, then return to a simmer before adding the chocolate.

# Chocolate-drenched cacao-nib cookies

There is always room in everyone's cooking repertoire for an awesome chocolate-chip cookie. I decided to create my own version of this classic by using pure cacao nibs and drenching the cooked biscuit in chocolate, giving a double hit of chocolate alongside the chewy center of the cookie. You will need to buy a padlock for your cookie jar as these are one of the most addictive biscuits you will ever eat. Cacao nibs are widely available online or from chocolate shops; alternatively, use chocolate chips, or even chopped almonds for a nutty version.

1 cup unsalted butter

¾ cup demerara sugar

Pinch of sea salt

1¾ cups all-purpose flour

scant 1 cup alkalized cocoa powder

½ vanilla pod, the seeds scraped out, or ½ teaspoon vanilla extract

1 large organic egg

50–100g cacao nibs (as many as you like), or chocolate chips

10½ ounces Venezuelan dark chocolate, or your favorite robust dark chocolate

Preheat the oven to 350°F.

Place the butter, sugar, and salt in a saucepan and melt thoroughly. Remove from the heat and add the flour, cocoa powder, vanilla seeds (or extract) and the egg, mixing thoroughly. Add the cacao nibs and allow the cookie dough to cool for 5 minutes.

On a parchment paper-lined baking sheet, place generous scoops of the dough, leaving 3 inches between each cookie. You'll probably need to bake in two or three batches. Bake for 8 to 10 minutes, then leave to cool completely.

Once you have baked your cookies and resisted eating them all while warm, the next step is to drench them in chocolate. Chop the dark chocolate into pieces. Temper the chocolate according to instructions on pages 18–21. Dip half of each cookie in the tempered chocolate and place back on the parchment paper to let the chocolate cool and set fully.

Store the cookies in an airtight container or leave on a plate for everyone to eat while fresh. They won't last long.

# Sea-salted caramel tart with Javanese milk chocolate

This tart, with its lusciously soft chocolate caramel filling, is adapted from a recipe for sea-salted caramels which won me my first ever chocolate award from the UK's Academy of Chocolate. Adding a touch of sea salt to chocolate or caramel is popular these days: the addition of a little salt balances sugar levels, intensifying the natural caramel taste and reducing the sugary feel of the caramel. You can try experimenting with different salts, as there are so many sea and rock salts on the market these days. *Fleur de sel,* the creme de la creme of French sea salts, is a favorite of mine. Whatever you do, steer clear of table salts as they are too chemical-tasting and not at all suitable for chocolate.

### FOR THE CRUST

½ cup unsalted butter, softened

¾ cups organic sugar

4 large organic egg yolks

3½ cups all-purpose flour

### FOR THE FILLING

14 tablespoons unsalted butter, softened

1 cup light muscovado sugar

1 cup heavy cream

1 teaspoon flaky sea salt, such as Maldon

7 ounces Javanese 40% milk chocolate, chopped

### FOR THE DECORATION

½ cup cracked cacao nibs

Preheat the oven to 350°F.

To make the pastry, first mix the butter and sugar together with a wooden spoon until smooth. Add the egg yolks and 1 tablespoon water and mix well. Then gradually add the flour to form a stiff dough. Wrap this in plastic wrap and refrigerate for 1 hour.

Roll out the chilled pastry to about ⅛ inch thick and use to line 4 tartlet tins. Bake blind for 25 minutes until golden and crisp.

For the filling, heat the butter and sugar in a large saucepan and simmer for 2 minutes. Add the cream and salt, then return to a boil and simmer for 5 minutes. Remove from the heat, then whisk in the chocolate until fully melted. Carefully pour the caramel into each tartlet shell and refrigerate until set.

To decorate and to add crunch, sprinkle the cacao nibs over the surface of the caramel.

# Sweet sandwich ganache

Most of us, at some point in our lives, have eaten a chocolate-spread sandwich. I have memories of thick slices of white bread stuck together with a layer of chocolate hazelnut spread, and I even recall mixing it into natural yogurt to create my own (but actually not very tasty) chocolate yogurt. So it seemed like a good idea to come up with a recipe for a chocolate spread to suit our discerning modern palates: a smooth, silky and indulgent ganache to spread on bread or cakes, or simply to eat from the jar.

3½ ounces Caribbean 66% dark chocolate

⅓ cup plus 1 tablespoon heavy cream

⅓ cup light muscovado sugar

Pinch of fine sea salt

5 teaspoons hazelnut oil, or other light nut oil

Chop the chocolate into small, even-sized pieces and place in a mixing bowl.

Put ⅓ cup plus 1 tablespoon water in a small pan, together with the cream, sugar and salt, bring to a boil and simmer for 2 minutes. Pour over the chocolate and mix well until smooth. Leave to cool for 30 minutes, then mix in the oil until emulsified and glossy.

Pour into sterilized jars and seal. Refrigerate and use within 2 weeks.

*Paul's top tip*
For a flavored spread, you can add your favorite spices to the creamy liquid in the pan. Adding a liqueur at the same time as the oil makes a wonderfully warming spread; whisky is especially delicious as its complex tastes and aromas pair well with the chocolate.

# Dark chocolate sorbet

It was 1980, we were having Sunday lunch at my Grandma's house, and were all full to bursting after many Yorkshire puddings. But, as anyone who knows me well will know, I have a separate stomach when it comes to desserts. On that day it was Neapolitan ice cream, consisting of layers of chocolate, strawberry and vanilla ice cream – lovely, except for the chocolate ice cream. To this day I am still not a big fan, as it doesn't usually taste of chocolate at all, and is often more like a bitter, powdery and artificially flavored frozen milkshake.

So I set out to find an alternative that *did* taste of chocolate, and had the color and intensity of dark chocolate without the bitterness. This recipe is smooth, rich and dairy-free, and is amazing on its own. Alternatively, try adding different liqueurs, herbs, or spices such as chile or cinnamon.

**1 cup plus 2 tablespoons organic sugar**

**1/3 cup alkalized cocoa powder**

**5 1/2 ounces 70% dark chocolate, chopped**

**3 tablespoons liqueur, such as Grand Marnier, Cognac or rum (optional)**

Bring a scant 2 cups water to a boil in a saucepan. Add the sugar, and cocoa powder and simmer for 3 minutes. Pour over the chocolate in a bowl and mix well. Allow to cool for 15 minutes, then add the liqueur, if using.

Once it has thoroughly cooled, churn the mixture in an ice-cream machine until smooth and silky. If you do not have an ice-cream maker, then place a freezer-proof container in the deep freeze for 30 minutes. Add the chocolate mixture, freeze for 30 minutes, then mix well with a fork or whisk. Repeat this process until you have a smooth, silky and frozen sorbet.

The sorbet can be stored for up to a month in the freezer.

*Paul's top tip*
If you prefer a firmer sorbet, reduce the amount of sugar or add a little less alcohol. Both sugar and alcohol inhibit the sorbet from freezing too firmly.

# 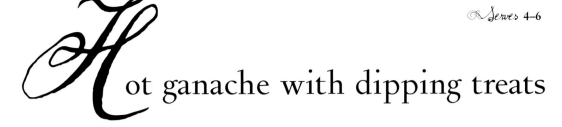ot ganache with dipping treats

Fondue is back in fashion and has been reinvented many times. My version is less liquid than many, and very glossy. It's perfect for a dinner-party dessert, with lots of sweet things to dip and share. Not only is the hot ganache fantastically quick to make, but also it has a wow factor that makes it look as though you have spent hours in the kitchen.

Be sure to tailor the dipping ingredients to the time of year, and I also recommend that you change the type of chocolate according to the season, in order to enjoy the dipped foods to the full. For example: 66% fragrant and delicate chocolate in spring; fruity Madagascan 64% chocolate in summer; 70% earthy chocolate in autumn; and 72–80% woody, robust and strong chocolate in winter.

**FOR THE GANACHE**

1 scant cup heavy cream

½ cup packed light muscovado sugar

Flavorings, such as cinnamon sticks, chile (powder or fresh), grated nutmeg, fresh basil, thyme, or lavender, or a liqueur (optional)

9 ounces dark chocolate, chopped

**FOR THE DIPPING TREATS**

**SPRING** – brownie cubes, marshmallows, banana, mini cookies

**SUMMER** – strawberries, cherries, brownie cubes, pineapple, mango, papaya

**AUTUMN** – peaches, apricots, pear, nectarines, mature Cheddar cubes, brownie cubes, plums

**WINTER** – Stilton cubes, dried figs, dates, brownie cubes, pear, dried apricots

**FOR THE DECORATION (OPTIONAL)**

orange zest, rose petals, lavender flowers and even chile slices all look great

Bring the cream and sugar to a boil and simmer for 1 minute, then remove from the heat and allow to rest for 2 minutes. If adding spices or herbs as flavoring, do so at this stage so that they infuse and scent the ganache fully.

Put the chocolate in a bowl, then pour over the cream mixture, whisking well to emulsify. The ganache should look glossy and very smooth. Pour into an attractive serving bowl and decorate if you wish.

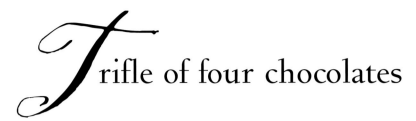

# Trifle of four chocolates

Are you like me in believing that the humble trifle is totally underrated? I adore trifle and would be very happy to eat it every day – as long as I made it myself, that is, as I am very particular about the jelly-to-cake and custard-to-cream ratios. This recipe, which includes four different chocolates, will reintroduce you to this classic dessert and is sure to become a staple dinner-party dessert or teatime treat. The recipe can be made as one large trifle or as individual portions in champagne or cocktail glasses.

### LAYER ONE: THE BOTTOM

About 11 ounces chocolate-brownie chunks (see page 58); store-bought brownies are OK, too

About cup whisky, sherry, rum, or coconut liqueur, for drizzling (optional)

### LAYER TWO: THE CHOCOLATE CREAM

18 ounces Javanese 40% milk chocolate, chopped

1²/₃ cups heavy cream

½ teaspoon flaky sea salt, such as Maldon

½ cup packed light muscovado sugar

### LAYER THREE: THE WHITE CHOCOLATE MOUSSE

11 ounces white chocolate

¾ cup heavy cream

### LAYER FOUR: THE SAUCE

¼ cup organic sugar

5½ ounces dark chocolate, chopped

### FOR DECORATION (OPTIONAL)

Chocolate, for grating

Chocolate pearls

For the first layer of trifle, place generous-sized brownie chunks in the bottom of the trifle bowl, making sure that the brownie can be seen through the bowl from the side. Drizzle over your favorite liqueur if you'd like to add a more adult flavor to the trifle.

To make the second layer, gently melt the milk chocolate in a hot water bath, mixing until smooth. Slowly warm the cream, salt and sugar in a sauce pan until lukewarm but not hot. Pour the warm cream into the milk chocolate and whisk together. Pour over the brownie chunks and place in the fridge to set.

To make the third layer of the trifle, gently melt the white chocolate in a hot water bath. Semi-whip the cream until soft and not stiff. Quickly fold the melted chocolate into the cream and pour onto the set milk-chocolate layer of the trifle. Place the trifle in the fridge to set.

For the final layer, bring ¹/₄ cup water and the sugar to a simmer in a pan, then pour onto the dark chocolate, mixing well. Allow the sauce to cool, then pour it over the white chocolate mousse layer. Place the trifle in the fridge for 30 minutes to set.

In terms of decoration, less can sometimes be more, and a simple decoration of finely chopped chocolate (perhaps a mix of dark, milk and white) can be enough to bring the dessert alive. Chocolate pearls are a good addition too, though more difficult to find. If you really want to gild the lily, a touch of edible silver or gold leaf will make this humble trifle into a show-stopping dessert.

# Paul's chocolate pudding extreme

Have you ever had one of those moments when only a chocolate pudding will do, when all you want to do is lock the doors, turn off the phone, and relax in front of your favorite movie eating something totally delicious and indulgent? Well, this is the quickest and easiest pudding you will ever make. It can be made in individual portions or as one large pudding. The steamed pudding with chocolate sauce is good enough, but adding a scoop of real vanilla ice cream on top of the pudding works wonders, too. The warm and cold temperatures balance well and create the perfect chocolate experience.

**FOR THE STEAMED PUDDING**

**4 cups all-purpose flour**

**1½ light muscovado sugar**

**1 cup unsalted butter, cut into tablespoons**

**¾ cup alkalized dark cocoa powder**

**3 tablespoons baking powder**

**1 teaspoon fine sea salt**

**6 large organic eggs**

**about ¼ cup milk**

**Softened unsalted butter, for greasing the bowls**

**FOR THE SAUCE**

**10½ ounces 70% dark chocolate**

**½ cup milk**

**¾ cup heavy cream**

**scant ½ cup light muscovado sugar**

**4 tablespoons unsalted butter, cut into small pieces**

Place the flour, brown sugar, butter, cocoa powder, baking powder and salt in a large mixing bowl. Rub together between your fingers until the mixture resembles breadcrumbs. Whisk the eggs lightly and add to the dry mixture, then mix well, gradually adding milk until the mixture forms a smooth batter.

Grease and flour a large (about 1-quart) pudding bowl, or several small (about ½ cup) individual basins. Fill with the mixture – filling small bowls to three-quarters full – then tap the bowl to level it. Cover the bowl or bowls tightly with three layers of plastic wrap. Place in a steamer or large saucepan with enough water to come halfway up the pudding bowls and simmer gently for 20–25 minutes.

You can make the sauce while the pudding's steaming. First, chop the chocolate and put into a bowl. Put the milk, cream and sugar in a saucepan and bring to a simmer, then pour over the chocolate and whisk well. Whisk in the butter until glossy and smooth.

The pudding will rise significantly, so when it is ready, lift it out of the steamer or pan, remove the plastic and, with a long sharp knife, slice off the excess pudding to create a level surface – you can nibble on the scrumptious steaming pudding tops.

Turn over the bowl and tap it sharply to release the pudding onto a plate. Serve immediately, smothered in the chocolate sauce: don't be shy with the sauce as you can never have too much.

If you are not eating the pudding immediately, allow it to cool and, when needed, simply steam it for 30 minutes or put it in the microwave on full power for 30–40 seconds.

# Three-chocolates christmas pudding

People often have a love-hate relationship with Christmas pudding. Whichever camp you fall into, here is an alternative that could change your life – or at least your Christmas – for ever. It is loaded with three different chocolates, but has a lighter texture than the traditional pudding, and is full of alternative dried fruits – dried figs, dates, apricots and cherries rather than sultanas, currants and raisins – soaked in copious amounts of booze. If you make only one Christmas pudding in your lifetime, then let it be this one. It also makes the perfect homemade Christmas present. Ideally, make the pudding no later than eight weeks before you're going to eat it.

1/3 diced dried apricots

2/3 cup diced dried figs

2/3 cup dates

2/3 cup dried cherries

2 tablespoons brandy

2 tablespoons port

1 teaspoon ground cinnamon

1 teaspoon ground cardamom

1/2 teaspoon freshly grated nutmeg

1/2 cup packed light muscovado sugar

5 tablespoons unsalted butter, softened

2 large organic eggs

1 1/3 cups all-purpose flour

1/4 cup alkalized cocoa powder

2 ounces 70% dark chocolate, broken into chunks

2 ounces white chocolate, broken into chunks

Generous 3/4 cup stout, such as Guinness

Juice and zest of 1 orange

Additional brandy, for storing the pudding

The night before making your pudding, put all the dried fruit, alcohol and spices in a bowl to soak.

In a large mixing bowl, cream together the sugar and butter. Gradually add the eggs until they are fully incorporated, then gradually mix in the flour, cocoa powder, and chocolate chunks. Add the Guinness, soaked fruits, orange juice, and zest and mix well – making a wish for the year ahead as you do so.

Grease and flour a 1.5-quart pudding basin before filling it with the pudding mixture. Place a buttered disc of parchment paper on top of the pudding, then wrap foil over the top of the bowl, securing it with string or an elastic band. Place in a steamer over simmering water, cover and steam for 3 hours. Do not allow the pan to boil dry: keep it topped up with boiling water from the kettle.

Once steamed, remove the pudding from the heat and leave it to cool overnight. The next day, wrap the pudding in a clean kitchen towel and store in the fridge.

Once a week, feed the pudding with one tablespoon of brandy: remove the foil and parchment paper and drizzle the brandy onto the surface. Cover the pudding over again and repeat weekly until serving. To reheat the pudding, place in a steamer for 90 minutes. Serve with brandy sauce, cream, or even ice cream.

*Makes* **about 16 biscuits, 30 if canapé-size**

# Chocolate water biscuits for cheese

**These unusual yet well-balanced crackers are the perfect pairing for many varieties of cheese, whether English, French, blue, goat or hard. You can give texture and extra flavor to the biscuits by adding dried herbs or spices such as fennel or cumin seeds, black pepper, or chile.**

- **2¼ cups plain flour**
- **1 teaspoon sea salt**
- **2 tablespoons cocoa powder**
- **½ teaspoon English mustard powder (optional)**
- **Your choice of spice or herb (optional)**
- **6 tablespoons unsalted butter**
- **⅓ cup ice-cold water, as needed**

Place all the flour, cocoa powder, and salt (including any flavorings) in a large bowl and mix well. Rub in the butter with your fingertips until evenly combined. Gradually add enough ice water to form a pliable dough; this must not be too sticky, so be careful when adding the water. Knead the dough gently until smooth. Wrap in plastic wrap and refrigerate for 30 minutes to rest and relax.

Preheat the oven to 350°F.

Roll the dough on a well-floured surface to ⅛ inch thick or thereabouts. Use a round cutter to cut out circles of your preferred size, e.g. a 1 inch cutter for canapé-size biscuits, or 2 inches for cheese biscuits; alternatively, use a sharp knife to cut into squares or rectangles. Prick each biscuit with a fork. Arrange on a baking sheet. Bake until golden and crisp, about 10–12 minutes. Place on a wire rack to cool.

The biscuits can be stored in an airtight container for 2–3 months.

# Fruit & Nuts

The pairing of chocolate with fruit or nuts is a classic combination found all over the world, and includes my favorite – chocolate-coated roast hazelnuts. In this chapter, I have included some classic recipes alongside some more contemporary ideas for combining chocolate with these two popular ingredients.

All nuts work well with a number of different types of chocolate. Roasting the nuts first is the best way to intensify their flavor. Raisins are a classic combination with dark chocolate, while the intense caramelized sugars of other naturally dried fruits, such as apricots, peaches and figs, can be stunning with milk chocolate. Remember to buy unsulphured dried fruits for their better flavor and appearance. And don't forget fresh fruits, which can give a particularly vibrant taste to chocolate – as in the first two recipes, for raspberry ganache and passion fruit and coconut truffles.

# Slow-roasted almond rocher slab with crimson raisins

I've taken the word "rocher" from the Swiss confection of roasted nuts bound in chocolate and presented in small stacks. If you like your chocolate robust, chunky, and with real bite, then this is for you. It is easy to make and you can adapt it to include your favorite nuts, dried fruits, seeds, and candied citrus peel. If you prefer you can cut the slab into bite-size pieces for a more dainty treat. Crimson raisins are slightly plumper, sweeter, and darker than golden ones, and can be found at well-stocked dried fruit and nut purveyors (see Suppliers).

**9 ounces nuts of your choice, chopped into even-sized pieces**

**⅔ cup crimson or golden raisins other dried fruit**

**10½ ounces dark chocolate of your choice, tempered**

Place the nuts on a baking sheet in a cold oven and turn the temperature to 350°F. When the oven is hot, set your timer to 5 minutes and watch the nuts while they roast, stirring now and again so that they roast evenly. Allow to cool thoroughly.

Mix 7 ounces of the nuts with the dried fruit and chocolate, mixing well and working with haste as the chocolate can set quickly at this stage. Pour the mixture onto a sheet of paper parchment, then place another sheet of paper on top. Use a rolling pin to roll the mixture to whatever thickness you fancy.

Allow the chocolate to cool until just set, then peel off the top parchment sheet. Sprinkle with the rest of the chopped nuts, then cut the slab into squares, rectangles or even triangles of your required size. Work quickly as the chocolate will harden and it is much easier to cut while soft. Alternatively, you can leave the chocolate to cool thoroughly and then break it into randomly shaped pieces.

Enjoy within 2 months of making – if it lasts that long!

# Honey and tahini ganache with toasted sesame seeds

Sesame seeds, when lightly toasted, complement chocolate incredibly well and add an amazing light, open texture to it. The addition of tahini (roasted sesame paste) intensifies the complexities and flavors in the finished chocolate. This is a fantastic after-dinner chocolate, and also goes exceptionally well with Moroccan, Egyptian and Algerian dishes.

**2½ tablespoons strong clover or heather honey**

**⅓ cup tahini**

**12½ ounces Caribbean 66% dark chocolate, chopped**

**¾ cup sesame seeds**

In a saucepan, bring a scant ¾ cup water and the honey to a simmer. Add the tahini and simmer for 2 minutes. Pour the hot liquid onto the chocolate in a bowl and whisk well until smooth. Allow to cool before refrigerating for at least 2 hours to fully set the ganache.

Lightly toast the sesame seeds in a dry frying pan until golden but not popping open. Leave to cool.

Take the ganache out of the fridge and, using a teaspoon, scoop out uneven quenelles and immediately roll them through the toasted sesame seeds.

Serve at room temperature and eat within 3 days.

# Salted pecan praline ganache

You will find that a chocolatier always has praline on the menu – usually his or her own secret recipe – as a good praline can be the best-selling chocolate in the business. My love affair with pralines began in the early 1980s, when I first tasted and fell for Thornton's foil-wrapped Diplomat chocolate and the famous Guylian sea shells. This is my favorite pecan praline recipe, and although the method requires patience I guarantee it is worth the wait. You can use the ganache to make rolled truffles or fill chocolate shells.

### FOR THE PRALINE PASTE

1 1/3 cups pecan halves

3/4 cup organic sugar

### FOR THE GANACHE

1 cup heavy cream

2/3 cup packed light muscovado sugar

1 teaspoon flaky sea salt, such as Maldon

10 ounces Javanese 40% milk chocolate, chopped

Preheat the oven to 350°F. Roast the pecans for 5 minutes, giving them a stir now and again to make sure that they roast evenly.

Heat a heavy-based saucepan (ideally copper), then sprinkle in a spoonful of the sugar and stir until it is fully melted. Add another spoonful and continue until all the sugar has been used up and is golden in color.

Add the warm pecans and mix well, then pour immediately onto parchment paper or a long-life rubber baking sheet and allow to cool thoroughly. Once cool and hard, break into small pieces and blend in a food processor until the pieces are small and oily. This can take up to 5 minutes, so remember to pause for a few seconds now and again so as not to burn out the motor.

Using a large mortar and pestle, crush one spoonful of praline at a time until it is as smooth as you can manage. Finally, push the paste through a sieve with a wooden spoon and place aside, covering until needed. This praline paste can be used just as it is in desserts, or keep a spoonful for later as it tastes amazing on crumpets or over ice cream.

To make the ganache, bring the cream, sugar and sea salt to a boil and simmer for 1 minute, then pour onto the chocolate in a bowl and whisk well. Add the praline paste and mix well. Allow to cool down enough to pipe into shells, or refrigerate and use to hand roll truffles.

# Hand-rolled wild strawberry and pink peppercorn truffles

Summer is a tricky time for chocolate as the humidity and heat shorten its shelf life dramatically. At this time of year, I always look for truly special and seasonal ingredients. *Fraises du bois* or French wild strawberries are a real treat, and we are lucky that imported wild strawberries are becoming more widely available; otherwise the best seasonal strawberries will do. I use white chocolate as the base for this ganache and add a sprinkling of crushed pink peppercorns to break the sweetness and add a tangy finish to the truffles. Serve them with delicate champagne or sparkling wine on a warm summer evening.

**FOR THE GANACHE**

**7 ounces wild strawberries**

**¼ cup organic sugar**

**1¾ cups heavy cream**

**3 tablespoons pink peppercorns, well crushed**

**1 pound white chocolate, chopped**

**Cornstarch or confectioners' sugar, for rolling**

**FOR COATING**

**10½ ounces white chocolate, chopped**

**3 tablespoons pink peppercorns, well crushed**

Wash the strawberries well, then place in a saucepan with the sugar and cook until puréed; you want the mixture to reduce by half to concentrate the flavor. Pass through a sieve to remove any lumps and fibers, return to the heat with the cream and peppercorns and simmer for 2 minutes. Pour on to the white chocolate in a bowl and blend well until smooth. Place in a container to cool, then refrigerate for at least 2 hours.

To roll the truffles: dust your hands with cornstarch, take even teaspoonfuls of the ganache and rapidly roll into spheres. Place the truffles onto parchment paper and put in the fridge to set.

To coat the truffles: temper the chocolate according to the instructions on pages 18–21. Dip the truffles into it, carefully coating them using your hands. Sprinkle with the crushed peppercorns immediately so that they stick to the chocolate. Place on paper parchment for 10 minutes to set.

# Ported plums roasted with orange in dark chocolate consommé

When summer slips into autumn and the first cool evenings mean an extra blanket on the bed, you know it's time for seasonal fruits, warming soups, and wholesome and satisfying foods. This recipe delivers on all counts, with roasted flavors, rich port and intense dark chocolate.

12 purple (Italian) plums

2 cups ruby port

1 cinnamon stick

Juice and zest of 4 oranges

2 cloves

1½ cups packed light muscovado sugar

**FOR THE CONSOMMÉ**

½ cup packed light muscovado sugar

11 ounces 70% dark chocolate, chopped

Orange zest, to decorate

Wash and dry the plums, then cut them in half and remove the pips. Soak the plums overnight in half the port, together with the cinnamon, orange juice and zest, sugar and cloves.

The next day, preheat the oven to 375°F. Place the plums, cut side up, on a baking sheet lined with paper parchment and roast for 15 minutes. Meanwhile, place the soaking juices with the remaining port in a saucepan and simmer until syrupy and reduced by half. Strain the syrup and discard the spices.

To make the consommé, bring 1 cup water and the sugar to a simmer, whisk in the chocolate and add the plum syrup.

Serve the plums in a shallow bowl with the warm consommé and shreds of orange zest.

# Passion-fruit and coconut truffles

A perfect summer chocolate – fresh, light and mouthwatering. The taste of the passion fruit could easily overpower the chocolate, so I have added coconut to temper and balance the fruit's flavor. This ganache is best piped into shells rather than rolled.

**16 passion fruits**

**¾ cup coconut milk**

**1¼ cups organic sugar**

**½ vanilla pod, the seeds scraped out**

**18 ounces Madagascan 64% dark chocolate or other fruity chocolate, chopped**

**About 50 chocolate shells and about 12 ounces tempered chocolate**

Make a purée out of the passion fruits. To do this, simply halve the fruit, scoop out the flesh and seeds into a sieve, then push the juice and flesh through until only the seeds remain. You should end up with about ²/₃ cup purée.

Bring the passion-fruit juice, coconut milk, sugar, vanilla seeds and 1 cup spring or filtered water to a boil and simmer for 2 minutes. Allow to cool for 2 minutes, then pour over the chocolate in a bowl and blend using a hand blender until smooth and glossy.

Fill the chocolate shells with the ganache and allow to set for at least 2 hours, then cap off with tempered chocolate. The shelf life of passion fruit is quite long, so your chocolates should last for 3 weeks in a cool, dry dark place.

*Serves 4–6*

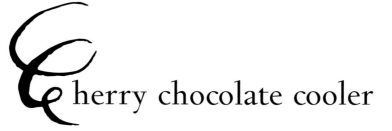

# Cherry chocolate cooler

This simple recipe for an ice-cold chocolate drink is transformed into the perfect long, summer cocktail by a shot of fruit liqueur. Feel free to use different fruits.

**¼ cup organic sugar**

**14 ounces 75% dark chocolate, chopped**

**Crushed ice**

**½ cup canned or pitted fresh cherries**

**⅓ cup liqueur, such as Kirsch, Crème de Cerise or Crème de Framboise**

Bring 2³/₄ cups water and the sugar to a simmer in a saucepan, then pour over the chocolate in a bowl and whisk well.

Half-fill a blender with crushed ice, add the chocolate liquid and the cherries and blend for 1 minute. Pour into glasses and spike with the liqueur of your choice.

# ried cherry and coconut brownie

The combination of dried sweet cherries, coconut and chocolate is stunning and this brownie improves with age. Sweet dried cherries match the dark chocolate beautifully, but sour dried cherries work well, too. (Be sure not to use candied cherries as they are too sweet.) I have never yet managed to eat just one bing cherry, and I advise any of you who manage to track them down not to share them with anyone!

**1 ¼ cups organic sugar**

**7 tablespoons unsalted butter**

**3 tablepoons golden syrup**

**10 ounces 70% dark chocolate, chopped**

**4 medium free-range eggs**

**⅔ cup unsweetened desiccated coconut**

**½ cup all-purpose flour (or spelt flour for a wheat-free brownie)**

**½ cup dried sweet cherries**

Preheat the oven to 325°F.

In a large saucepan, melt the sugar and butter and syrup until smooth. Remove from the heat and add the chocolate, stirring until melted. Whisk the eggs and beat into the chocolate mixture. Add the coconut and flour and mix thoroughly.

Pour into a greased pan (6 x 8 x 1 inch) lined with parchment paper and spread evenly. Scatter the cherries evenly across the top of the brownie. Bake for 20 minutes, or until set around the edges. Remove from the oven, cool and refrigerate overnight.

Turn out of the pan, remove the paper and trim the edges off the brownie. Using a wet knife, cut the brownie into whatever-size squares you wish. Serve at room temperature or warm.

The brownies will keep for 4 days in an airtight container in the fridge.

# Maple macadamia ganache

All I am going to say is yum yum yum!

**7 ounces Madagascan 50% milk chocolate, chopped**

**3½ tablespoons pure maple syrup**

**FOR THE DECORATION**

**2 cups organic sugar**

**24 macadamia nuts**

Bring ⅓ cup water to a simmer and pour over the milk chocolate in a bowl, mixing well to create a ganache. Allow to cool thoroughly, then stir the maple syrup through lightly to give a ripple effect.

Spoon the ganache into something imaginative to serve. I like to use unusual receptacles to serve my desserts, such as mini jars, unusual glasses, or teacups.

Melt the sugar in a saucepan and cook until a rich golden caramel color. Spoon eight lines onto parchment paper and immediately place three macadamias in a line onto each line of caramel so that they set in place. When cool, remove from the parchment and place across the top of each glass of ganache.

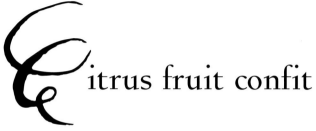

# Citrus fruit confit

These jewel-like chocolates are a labor of love, and can take two or three days to crystallize and set, but they are definitely worth the wait. Always use thick-skinned citrus fruits, such as navel oranges, pink grapefruit, and large lemons and limes. You can make as many or as few as you like depending on how much fruit you choose to use. I suggest starting with one or two fruits for your first go. You are bound to end up with more chocolate than you need, but 12 ounces is the minimum amount that can be tempered.

## FOR THE CONFIT

**1 grapefruit makes up to 30 chocolates**

**1 orange makes up to 20 chocolates**

**1 lemon makes 20 to 25 chocolates**

**1 lime makes 10 to 15 chocolates**

## FOR THE STOCK SYRUP

**2½ cups organic sugar**

## FOR DIPPING

**Minimum of 10½ ounces tempered dark chocolate, but the quantity will depend on the number of truffles you are making**

### Paul's top tip
**Feel free to flavor your sugar syrup with spices such as cinnamon, nutmeg or cardamom. Liqueurs can add intensity and warmth.**

Prepare the fruit by first washing it thoroughly. Score through the outer skin from the top of the fruit to the bottom until you reach the flesh. Repeat this four times, then use your thumb to work the skin from the flesh in four or five separate pieces. If you like chunky pieces of fruit, cut each skin segment in half lengthways, or for a thinner, more delicate chocolate, cut the pieces into four.

Bring a pan of water to a boil and simmer the strips of skin for 3 minutes. Strain and repeat twice. The reason to do this is to extract the bitterness from the skin. For grapefruit you should repeat the process 3 times as the skin can be very bitter.

Make the syrup, by bringing 1¾ cups water and the sugar to a boil in a large saucepan, stirring occasionally to dissolve the sugar. Place the cooked fruit strips into the hot syrup and simmer very gently for 3 hours. Do not rush the cooking by increasing the heat as this will caramelize the syrup and the fruits will become too toffee-like.

Once cooked, the fruit will look translucent and feel very soft. Allow to cool in the syrup overnight as is. Carefully strain the fruit from the syrup – the strips will be very fragile, so take care. (Save the syrup; it can be churned into sorbet or used again for your next batch of fruit confit.) Place on a wire rack for 24 hours or until the sugars have crystallized and dried.

Using your fingers, dip the confits in your desired chocolate so they are half-coated. If you want to fully coat them with chocolate, use a dipping fork instead of your fingers. Place on parchment paper to set.

The chocolates can be kept in an airtight container for up to 3 months, but I bet you'll have eaten them all within a day or two.

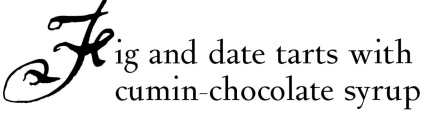

# Fig and date tarts with cumin-chocolate syrup

These individual triangular, free-form tarts use my favorite type of pastry, made with cream cheese. It is wonderfully light, flaky and buttery, and melts in the mouth. What's more, cream-cheese pastry is infinitely versatile and the quickest pastry you can make – I promise. There is no baking blind or tart pan required, so it's a useful technique to have in your repertoire for making all kinds of beautiful tarts.

**FOR THE CREAM CHEESE PASTRY**

1 cup plus 2 tablespoons unsalted butter, at room temperature

10 ounces cream cheese, at room temperature

1 teaspoon vanilla extract

2¼ cups all-purpose flour

1 egg yolk, for glazing

**FOR THE FILLING**

6–8 firm fresh figs

12–18 Medjool dates, pitted

Demerara sugar, for sprinkling

**FOR THE CUMIN-CHOCOLATE SYRUP**

½ cup organic sugar

5 teaspoons cumin seeds

7 ounces 70% dark chocolate, chopped

With a wooden spoon, cream together the butter, cream cheese and vanilla until smooth and fully mixed. Gradually stir in the flour to form a dough; use a mixer if this becomes heavy work. Wrap the pastry in plastic wrap and refrigerate for 2 hours until set and quite firm.

Dust plenty of flour over the work surface, then divide tthe dough into 4 larger pieces or 6 more modest-sized pieces and roll each to ⅛-inch thick. Use a saucer or large metal cutter to cut out rounds. Brush each disc with egg, then roll one section of the perimeter in to form a rolled edge, then turn the disc a third of a turn and roll again, then repeat for the final side. This forms the sides of your three-point tart. Brush the tart shells with the remaining egg yolk and refrigerate for 10 minutes.

Preheat the oven to 350°F.

To make the filling, trim the figs and cut in half. Place one fig half, cut side up, in each corner of a tart and a date between each fig half. Sprinkle liberally with demerara sugar. Bake for 20–25 minutes until golden and crisp.

For the chocolate syrup, bring ⅓ cup water, the sugar and cumin seeds to a boil and simmer for 5 minutes until the cumin has infused the syrup fully. Strain the seeds out, add to the chocolate in a bowl, and whisk until melted and smooth.

Serve the tarts warm or at room temperature with the cumin-chocolate syrup drizzled over the top.

# White chocolate goat cheese cheesecake with raspberry compote

I adore a good cheesecake, but only if it has the right texture, taste, and lots of fruit and, of course, chocolate. I created this recipe one hot and balmy summer evening when I wanted something sweet yet refreshing, and not in the least bit heavy. Use a mild, rindless goat cheese and vary the fruit according to the season or indeed your taste. Serve with a glass of sparkling wine laced with elderflower liqueur.

## FOR THE CHEESECAKE

1 cup chocolate cookies

5 tablepoons unsalted butter

2 tablespoons demerara sugar

11 ounces rindless goat cheese

7 ounces cream cheese

1¾ cups organic sugar

3 large organic eggs

Zest and juice of 1 lemon

2 tablespoons cornstarch

5½ ounces white chocolate, chopped

## FOR THE RASPBERRY COMPOTE

10 ounces raspberries

½ cup organic sugar

1 teaspoon rosemary leaves

Zest and juice of 1 lemon

To make the base for the cheesecake, crush the cookies to the size of fine breadcrumbs and put in a bowl. Melt the butter and stir into the cookie crumbs, then add the demerara sugar and mix well. Press the crumb mixture into a greased 8-inch springform pan and allow to cool.

Let the goat and cream cheese come to room temperature in a large bowl. Add the sugar, eggs, lemon zest and juice, and mix until smooth and lump-free. Add the cornstarch and mix well.

Preheat the oven to 300°F.

Melt the chocolate carefully in a hot water bath. Slowly pour into the cheese mixture and whisk well. Pour into the pan and carefully place on a baking sheet. Bake for 1 hour or until the top is lightly golden. The cheesecake should still be slightly soft and have a wobble to the center when baked. Do not overbake or the cake will crack; overcooking can also give the filling a greeny-gray hue.

Allow the cheesecake to cool thoroughly. Refrigerate in the pan for at least 2 hours.

To make the compote, cook the raspberries, sugar, rosemary leaves, lemon zest, and juice over a saucepan over very low heat until soft and deep red in color. Cool to room temperature.

To serve: remove the cheesecake from the pan and place on a serving plate. Use a hot wet knife to cut perfect and generous wedges, and spoon the compote over the top.

# Fresh raspberry ganache with black raspberry liqueur

This was one of the very first chocolates I ever created and is still one of my favorites. The finished ganache is very soft and will need to be piped into a chocolate shell rather than rolled. Eat within 3 weeks.

½ cup organic sugar

7 ounces fresh raspberries

½ cup heavy cream

10½ ounces Madagascan 64% dark chocolate, broken into pieces

1½ tablespoons Chambord (black raspberry liqueur)

About 50 chocolate shells and 12 ounces tempered chocolate

Mix together the sugar and raspberries and allow to stand for at least 4 hours at room temperature.

Purée the raspberries with a hand blender, then pass the pulp through a sieve into a saucepan. Add the cream and $1/3$ cup spring or filtered water, bring to a boil, and simmer for 2 minutes. Remove from the heat and leave to rest for 2 minutes.

Put the chocolate in a bowl, pour in the hot liquid, and blend with a whisk or hand blender. Allow to cool thoroughly. Mix in the raspberry liqueur. Pipe the ganache into chocolate shells, and seal with tempered chocolate.

# Black currant and licorice truffles

This was inspired by a type of sweet I used to love as a child, the one with a hard outer shell and a black currant and licorice toffee center. This ganache is very soft and must be used to fill chocolate shells.

3 sticks licorice root

1 cup packed light muscovado sugar

11 ounces black currants, fresh or jarred

1 pound Venezuelan 72% dark chocolate, or another robust and strong chocolate

3½ tablespoons Crème de Mûres (blackberry liqueur)

About 40 chocolate shells and 12 ounces tempered chocolate

Put $3/4$ cup spring or filtered water in a pan with the licorice roots, bring to a boil, and simmer for 6 minutes. Allow to cool thoroughly. Cover, then leave to infuse overnight.

The next day, strain out the sticks and return the water to the heat, adding the sugar and black currants. Simmer for 5 minutes. Purée with a hand blender and strain to remove any seeds and skin from the fruit.

Chop the chocolate, add to the liquid, and blend until smooth. Add the Crème de Mûres and the ganache is ready. Fill the chocolate shells, then allow to set for 2 hours. Eat within 5 days.

# Rosemary-poached pears with Stilton ganache and walnuts

This recipe may sound a little strange at first – and it should certainly trigger some interesting conversations – but in fact the flavors and textures balance together very well. As far as your taste buds are concerned, mature Stilton and dark intense chocolate have a similar flavor profile, so when eaten or blended together their flavors marry perfectly without one's overpowering the other.

**FOR THE PEARS**

4 firm Bartlett pears

6 long stalks of rosemary

1 x 750ml bottle sweet white wine

1 lemon, cut in half

**FOR THE GANACHE**

7 ounces 70% dark chocolate, chopped

1 cup heavy cream

3 ounces soft, ripe Stilton

**FOR SERVING**

1 tablespoon toasted chopped walnuts

1 ounces Stilton, crumbled

4 mint leaves

Peel and core the pears, leaving the fruits whole and the stalks intact. To do this, push a corer halfway up into the bottom of the pear, twist and then pull out; then use a teaspoon to scoop out the core.

Place the pears in a saucepan. Bruise the rosemary with a rolling pin. Add to the pan with the wine and lemon halves. Cover and simmer for 20 minutes until the pears are tender.

Remove from the heat and allow the pears to marinate until cooled. Then carefully remove the pears from the pan and place on kitchen towels for 5 minutes to soak up any excess liquid.

Strain the cooking liquid into a clean saucepan and simmer until it is reduced to a thick syrup. This may take up to 30 minutes, but what is left is a wonderfully aromatic and fragrant rosemary syrup to serve with the pears.

Now for the ganache. Place the chocolate and heavy cream in a hot water bath and stir until glossy, making sure that all the chocolate has melted. Break the Stilton into small pieces and whisk into the chocolate mixture until smooth and once again glossy. Remove from the heat and set aside.

Preheat the oven to 400°F. Stand the pears on a baking sheet lined with parchment paper. Roast for 15 minutes, remove, and let stand for 5 minutes.

Holding a pear by its stalk, plunge it into the Stilton ganache at an angle to half-coat the pear, and place on a serving plate. Spoon some of the rosemary syrup on the plate, sprinkle with some roasted walnuts Stilton, too. Using a wooden toothpick, make a hole in the top of the pear and push in a mint leaf to finish.

# Chocolate and almond tortellini with blood oranges and pine nuts

One of my favorite pasta recipes, and it's a dessert! The bitter chocolate dough, creamy almond filling and zesty blood-orange sauce balance beautifully to make a really show-stopping pudding. The best part is that everything can be prepared in advance so you can easily put the dessert together for a dinner party.

**FOR THE PASTA DOUGH**

2½ cups semolina pasta flour

½ cup alkalized cocoa powder

2 large organic eggs

1 tablespoon almond oil (or other nut oil)

**FOR THE FILLING**

4 tablespoons unsalted butter

½ cup granulated sugar

⅔ cup whole milk

½ vanilla pod, the seeds scraped out (save the pod to make vanilla sugar)

6 amaretti cookies, crushed

1 large organic egg

1 large organic egg yolk, beaten, for sealing the tortellini

3 tablespoons all-purpose flour

¼ cup almond flour

3 tablespoons Amaretto liqueur

**FOR THE BLOOD-ORANGE SAUCE**

4 blood oranges

⅓ cup organic sugar

1½ cups heavy cream

**FOR THE DECORATION**

⅓ cup pine nuts, toasted

A few basil leaves, thinly sliced

For the pasta dough, place all the ingredients, along with 2 tablespoons cold water, in a food processor and process until a soft but firm dough has formed. Alternatively, mix the dough by hand in a large mixing bowl. Wrap in plastic wrap and put in the fridge for 30 minutes.

Using a pasta machine, roll the dough into thin sheets and cut out circles using a 4-inch cutter. If you don't have a pasta machine, use a rolling pin. Lay the pasta discs on a plate, cover and refrigerate until ready to fill.

To make the filling, cream the butter and sugar in a bowl, then simply add the rest of the ingredients and mix well. To fill the pasta, take a pasta disc and wet the edges with the egg yolk. Place a teaspoon of the filling in the center. Fold the disc over and pinch the edges together to form a half-moon shape. Holding the filled pasta in both hands, with the straight edge at the bottom, bring each corner together and pinch, forming a parcel. Repeat for all the discs and store the finished tortellini in the fridge until needed.

For the sauce, zest the oranges using a fine grater. Then peel and divide the oranges into segments, doing this over a bowl so as to save all the juice. Make a stock syrup by bringing 3 tablespoons water and the sugar to a boil in a large saucepan, stirring occasionally to dissolve the sugar. Add the reserved juice and the zest, bring to a boil and simmer for 2 minutes. Add the cream and simmer for a minute more. Remove from the heat and add the orange segments.

Bring a large pan of water to a brisk simmer. Drop in the tortellini and simmer for 3 minutes or until they float on the surface. Remove and drain. Divide the tortellini between serving bowls, then spoon over the blood-orange sauce and segments. Decorate with the toasted pine nuts and sliced basil.

# Sea-salted chocolate and pecan tart

Definitely one for a special dinner party. With its sophisticated, sweet chocolate pastry crust, unctuous ganache filling, and caramelizd salted pecans, this tart will stop all conversation for all the right reasons.

### FOR THE CRUST

12 tablespoons unsalted butter

1/3 cup organic sugar

2 egg large organic yolks

1 3/4 all-purpose flour

3 tablespoons alkalized cocoa powder

### FOR THE FILLING

7 ounces Madagascan 64% dark chocolate, broken into pieces

1 cup packed light muscovado sugar

3/4 cup heavy cream

1 tablespoon flaky sea salt, such as Maldon

### FOR THE TOPPING

1/2 cup granulated sugar

1 teaspoon Maldon sea salt

1 cup pecan halves

To make the crust, cream together the butter and sugar with a wooden spoon until light and creamy. Add the egg yolks and 2 tablespoons water and mix well until all the liquid has been incorporated. Gradually add the flour and cocoa powder until a paste is formed. This can all be done in an electric mixer or food processor if you prefer.

Wrap the pastry in plastic wrap, flatten into a disk, and refrigerate for 1 hour. The pastry can be made 2 days ahead, or even longer since it freezes well, though in this case, thaw and knead the pastry to soften it before rolling.

Sprinkle the work surface with flour and roll out the pastry until it is about 2 inches bigger than your tart pan. I recommend using a ring that is 10 inches in diameter and 1 inch deep.

Carefully line the pan, pushing the pastry well into the bottom edges and folding the excess over the top. Trim off the excess. Refrigerate for 15 minutes to relax the pastry and to help prevent it from shrinking during cooking.

Preheat the oven to 350°F. Line the tart with a sheet of parchment paper – scrunch it up first to soften it – then fill with dried beans, lentils, or raw rice, bake blind for 20 minutes. Lift out the beans and bake for 5–8 minutes more, until the shell is dry. Allow to cool.

To make the filling, put all the ingredients in a heatproof mixing bowl – place it over a pan of very hot water and allow them to melt together until glossy and thick. Pour into the cooled, baked crust and refrigerate for 2 hours.

For the topping, heat a saucepan until warm and gradually add the sugar, stirring until you have a golden liquid caramel. Add the salt and mix well. Pour in the pecans and, mixing thoroughly, quickly pour the mixture onto a parchment paper and spread out with a spatula. Allow to cool thoroughly, then break or chop up into shards or chunky pieces to sprinkle over the ganache.

Cut the tart with a hot, wet knife for perfect, restaurant-quality slices. Serve alone with a glass of Banyuls or Maury wine.

# Sugar & Spice

And everything nice! With this chapter I wanted to
share with you the versatile and often forgotten
ingredients in chocolate- and dessert-making. We use
sugar and spices in a huge variety of recipes but they are
often secondary ingredients rather than the highlight
of the dish. I try to let the spices shine in my recipes,
and always include the most significant ones in the name
of the dish. In terms of sugar, of the numerous types
available, I choose to use organic unrefined sugars,
particularly organic sugar and the toffee-flavored
muscovado sugar. Changing the sugar you use will
completely change the flavor of your finished chocolate.

# Cacao-nib and Madagascan vanilla smoothie

This recipe takes two minutes from beginning to end and it will give you an amazing lift. Try it!

2 tablespoons cacao nibs

Scant 1 cup 1% milk, soy milk or rice milk

Scant 1 cup thick Greek yogurt

Seeds of ½ Madagascan vanilla pod, or 1 teaspoon vanilla extract

1 tablespoon clover honey

Place all the ingredients in a blender and process until the cacao nibs have ground to small pieces. It is as simple as that! Enjoy.

# Pantry tea truffles

Here's a recipe that uses any type of tea that you might have lying around, such as camomile, peppermint, Assam, Earl Grey, Darjeeling, Lapsang Souchong, English breakfast, rooibos, or even a fruit tea.

4–6 tablespoons loose tea (depending on its strength)

½ organic sugar

18 ounces Caribbean 66% dark chocolate, or another delicate dark chocolate

You need to make a very, very strong infusion of your chosen tea, as the chocolate will overpower the delicate flavors if the tea is too weak. I use about 4 tablespoons of loose tea per 1 cup water, or more if I am using a delicate tea.

Bring 1 cup water, the tea and sugar to a boil and simmer for 3 minutes. Take off the heat and leave to infuse until cold. Strain through a very fine sieve or cheese cloth, then bring back to a simmer.

Chop the chocolate and put in a bowl. Add the infused tea, whisking well. Now taste the ganache for the strength of tea flavors and aromas. Some can be intensified with essential oils, such as bergamot for Earl Grey, jasmine oil for jasmine tea, peppermint and so on. You can also strengthen the flavor by adding a small amount of very strong tea, but remember to adjust the chocolate quantity if adding a lot more liquid.

Allow the ganache to cool and pipe into shells, or refrigerate and roll into truffles when set.

# Muscovado truffles

This is my favorite quick and easy truffle recipe and perfect for last-minute gifts or dinner parties. It is wonderfully smooth, with the depth of caramel and sticky toffee pudding and a long, lingering fragrance from the chocolate.

**6 tablespoons packed light muscovado sugar**

**Scant 1 cup heavy cream**

**Pinch of fine sea salt**

**9 ounces 70% dark chocolate, chopped**

**FOR ROLLING**

**½ cup alkalized cocoa powder**

**3 tablespoons light muscovado sugar**

Bring the sugar, cream and salt to a simmer. Pour over the chocolate in a heatproof bowl and whisk well until emulsified and glossy. Let the ganache cool, then refrigerate.

When you are ready to roll the truffles, mix the cocoa powder and sugar together well until fully combined. Now, take a generous amount of the ganache and, having dipped your hands into the dry mixture, form your desired sphere – or feel free to give the truffles a rustic shape.

Once shaped, re-roll the truffles through the dry powder to coat them. Store in an airtight container in the fridge – or even the freezer if you want a constant supply of emergency truffles. But be sure to let them come to room temperature before eating.

**Variations**
Here are another couple of ideas for ways to enjoy your truffles:

Bring a mugful of milk to a simmer, place one muscovado truffle in the bottom of your cup, then pour on the hot milk and allow to stand for 2 minutes. You can either drink the warm milk and enjoy the molten chocolate at the bottom, or give everything a good stir for a soothing hot chocolate.

Skewer the truffles onto toothpicks and refrigerate. Melt a small bowl of your favorite chocolate over a saucepan of hot water until smooth. Place your truffles around the dish of melted chocolate, then dip and indulge.

# Chocolate ginger and cardamom tea bread

Dark chocolate and stem ginger are perfect partners in every possible way. In this recipe I have used the classic combination but added deep, earthy cardamom and strong Assam tea. The result is a moist loaf cake packed with juicy pieces of stem ginger, handfuls of chocolate chunks and a caramely muscovado top.

**9 ounces crystallized stem ginger**

**²/₃ cup seedless raisins**

**2 teaspoons ground cardamom**

**Zest of 1 orange**

**6 tablespoons packed light muscovado sugar**

**²/₃ cup plus 1 tablespoon strong brewed Assam tea**

**1 large organic egg, beaten**

**1¹/₃ cups self-rising flour**

**3¹/₂ ounces 70% dark chocolate, coarsely chopped**

Place the ginger, raisins, sugar, cardamom, and orange zest into a small mixing bowl and pour in the hot tea. Cover and let soak for about 8 hours.

Preheat the oven to 325°F.

Add the beaten egg to the fruit mixture, followed by the flour, and mix well. Add the chocolate and mix again. Pour the mixture into a 8 by 4-inch loaf pan lined with parchment paper, and bake for 1¹/2 hours.

Cool the cake in the pan for 30 minutes, then carefully remove from the pan, discarding the paper. Wrap the cake in fresh parchment paper and a kitchen towel for 24 hours before eating.

Serve with soft butter and a real hot chocolate (see page 34).

# Venezuelan chocolate pancakes with chocolate maple syrup

This recipe is my homage to Sunday-morning brunch, which is one of those occasions when anything goes; in other words, be as indulgent and naughty as you like because it is certainly not the time to count calories or grams of fat. Feel free to add blueberries, nuts, and sultanas if the fancy takes you. The syrup can be made days or even weeks in advance and stored in the fridge.

## FOR THE PANCAKES

1 ounce Venezuelan 100% (unsweetened) dark chocolate, grated

1 1/3 cups buckwheat or spelt flour

1 large organic egg

1/3 cup plus 1 tablespoon light muscovado or brown sugar

1 cup plus 3 tablespoons milk

2 teaspoons baking soda

1 teaspoon vanilla extract

unsalted butter, melted, as needed

## FOR THE SYRUP

Pinch of sea salt

Scant 1 cup pure maple syrup

3 1/2 ounces 70% dark chocolate, chopped

Place all the pancake ingredients (except the butter) in a blender or food processor and process until a smooth, thick batter is formed. Leave the batter to rest while you make the syrup.

To make the syrup, dissolve the salt in 2 tablespoons water in a saucepan over a gentle heat, then add the maple syrup and bring to a simmer. Pour over the chocolate in a heatproof bowl and whisk well until smooth.

Heat a crêpe pan or nonstick large frying pan until quite hot and grease with butter. Spoon 1/4-cup portions of the batter into the griddle, spacing them well apart. Cook over medium heat until you see bubbles on the surface of the pancake, then carefully turn over and cook for another 1–2 minutes. Place the pancakes on a plate and cover with foil until you have cooked the entire batch.

Serve the pancakes laced with the warm syrup – be generous as the pancakes soak up a lot!

# Ancho chile with lime truffles

That chile and chocolate make a great combination was discovered back in the time of the Aztec, Olmec Indian and Mayan cultures. Over the past ten years, there has been a global revival of the chile-and-chocolate marriage, and this truffle is my particular favorite.

**¹/₃ cup heavy cream**

**¹/₂ cup packed light muscovado sugar**

**1 teaspoon pure ground ancho chile powder, or your own choice**

**Grated zest of 1 lime**

**7 ounces 70% dark chocolate, chopped**

Bring ¹/₃ cup water, the cream, sugar, chile, and lime zest to boil and simmer for 2 minutes. Remove from the heat and infuse until cooled. Taste to test how hot the chile is; if you find the heat too fierce, add a little more sugar, or, if you prefer more heat, put in some ground chile. Strain.

Bring the liquid back to a simmer, cool for a minute, then pour over the chocolate in a heatproof bowl and whisk well until glossy. You can either use the ganache straight away to fill chocolate shells, or cool and roll into the classic truffle ball shape.

# Aztec spiced truffles

The Aztecs drank copious amounts of cocoa in a cold, frothy form flavored with cinnamon, chile and nutmeg. Today, I make my Aztec hot chocolate in the same way (see page 34), using water instead of milk or cream and by infusing warming spices into the liquid. This recipe for a spiced truffle is also water-based.

½ cinnamon stick

¼ teaspoon pure ground ancho chile

½ fresh nutmeg, grated

⅓ cup packed light muscovado sugar

7 ounces African 85% dark chocolate, chopped

**FOR COATING**

1⅓ cups alkalized cocoa powder

1 teaspoon ground cinnamon

½ teaspoon grated fresh nutmeg

9 ounces 70% dark chocolate, tempered

Put ⅔ cup water in a pan with the cinnamon stick, chile, nutmeg, and sugar, bring to a boil and simmer for 5 minutes. Strain over the chocolate in a heatproof bowl and whisk well until smooth. Cool, pour into a shallow dish, and refrigerate for at least 1 hour.

For the coating, combine the cocoa powder and spices in a medium-size bowl, mixing well.

Scoop and roll the ganache between your fingertips until you have even-sized spheres. Now dip your hands into the tempered chocolate and carefully roll each truffle in your hands until fully coated. As you coat one, immediately roll it through the cocoa mixture and transfer to parchment paper and let set fully.

# Gingerbread-spice ganache

This is a perfect autumn and winter chocolate. Gingerbread is most popular at Christmas time, so these truffles make a great Christmas gift, especially when packed creatively in a large glass jar or handmade box.

1 tablespoon molasses

1 cup heavy cream

¾ cup packed light muscovado or brown sugar

3½ ounces crystallized ginger, minced

2 teaspoons ground ginger

1¼ pounds Javanese 40% milk chocolate, chopped

About 10½ ounces milk chocolate, tempered

**FOR COATING**

Ground ginger, nutmeg and cinnamon (optional)

Bring ⅓ cup water, cream, sugar and crystallized ground ginger, and molasses to a boil in a saucepan. Simmer for 2 minutes. Give the mixture a good stir for 30 seconds. Add the chocolate and stir until all the chocolate has melted. Pour into a plastic container and chill until fully set.

Roll the ganache into even-sized spheres, coat in the tempered chocolate, and decorate as desired. A simple mixture of ground ginger, nutmeg and cinnamon is perfect, sprinkled onto each truffle before the chocolate has set.

# uscovado chocolate cakes with cacao nibs and Mayan spiced syrup

My name is Paul A. Young and I am a cake-a-holic. I cannot imagine my life without this humble cake, whether it's for afternoon tea, a quick coffee break or a stolen hour gossiping with friends. Moist and sticky with crunchy cacao nibs and an aromatic sweet-spiced syrup, these cakes are the perfect dessert served warm with real vanilla ice cream or cold with rooibos or Earl Grey tea.

**FOR THE CAKES**

¾ cup self-rising flour

⅔ cup alkalized cocoa powder

½ teaspoon fine sea salt

13 tablespoons unsalted butter, cut up

1 cup plus 1 tablespoon packed light muscovado or brown sugar

⅓ cup heavy cream

2 medium free-range eggs

Scant ½ cup cracked cacao nibs

**FOR THE SYRUP**

1 cup organic sugar

½ fresh nutmeg, grated

1 cinnamon stick, broken in half

¼ teaspoon pure ground ancho chile powder

Preheat the oven to 350°F.

Place the flour, cocoa, salt and butter in a large mixing bowl. Rub between your fingers until the mixture has the consistency of breadcrumbs. Add the sugar and mix well.

Whisk 6 tablespoons water with the cream and eggs. Pour into the dry mixture. Mix until smooth.

For the cupcakes, you can either use shop-bought paper cases or, for a more contemporary style, make them yourself using nonstick paper parchment: cut 6-inch squares of parchment paper, scrunch them up tight in your hand, then open them out just enough to fit into the muffin cups.

Fill each case three-quarters full with cake battter and sprinkle each with plenty of cocoa nibs. Bake for 12–15 minutes, or until springy to the touch. Remove from the muffin pan and place on a wire rack to cool.

To make the sugar syrup, bring ⅔ cup water, the sugar and all the spices to a boil and simmer for 5 minutes. Remove from the heat and infuse for 15 minutes. Strain through a sieve into a liquid measuring cup.

While the cupcakes are still warm, slowly and gradually moisten each one with an even amount of syrup until glossy, allowing the syrup to soak fully into the cakes. If serving as a plated dessert, reserve some syrup to drizzle over and around each cake.

# Salt and pepper ganache

The idea for this ganache came to me at my favorite Thai restaurant while I was eating a rather overwhelming plate of salt and pepper squid. I loved the balance of the warming pepper and tangy sea salt combined with the delicate sweetness of the squid. So I decided to transpose this into a ganache that can be used either to make truffles or as a dipping sauce for fruits such as pineapple, mango and strawberry – all of which benefit from a little salt and pepper.

¼ cup packed light muscovado sugar

1 teaspoon flaky sea salt, such as Maldon

½ teaspoon freshly ground black pepper

10½ ounces fine 66% dark chocolate, chopped

Bring a scant ³/4 cup water to a simmer with the sugar and salt in a saucepan. Remove from the heat while you toast the pepper.

Lightly toast the pepper in a dry frying pan over medium heat until you can smell the aromatic essential oils being released. Take care not to overtoast the pepper as it will become bitter. Add the pepper to the liquid in the pan and return to a simmer for 2 minutes. Pour over to the chocolate in a heatproof bowl and whisk well until smooth.

Use the ganache while warm as a dipping sauce, or refrigerate and then roll into truffles. The ganache can be stored in the fridge for up to 5 days in an airtight container.

# Ginger and fennel-seed truffles

The balance of flavor in this chocolate is truly wonderful and I never tire of its sparkle and tingle on the tongue. Chinese stem ginger has a wonderful perfume and can be found at Asian grocers.

**⅔ cup heavy cream**

**3½ ounces crystallized ginger slices**

**¼ cup packed light muscovado or brown sugar**

**3 tablespoons fennel seeds**

**10½ ounces Javanese 40% milk chocolate, chopped**

**About 40 milk chocolate shells and 10½ ounces tempered chocolate**

Heat the cream, ginger, sugar, and fennel seeds in a saucepan and simmer for 3 minutes. Remove from the heat and infuse for 15 minutes. Puree using a hand blender or standard kitchen blender until the ginger pieces are small and evenly sized; this helps to release the intense flavors.

With a wooden spoon or the back of a ladle, push the liquid and pulp through a sieve, and discard the dry solids in the sieve. Bring the liquid back to a simmer, then whisk in the chocolate until smooth and glossy. Cool for 30 minutes. Use to fill pre-made truffle shells then close with the tempered chocolate.

# Toasted cumin and coriander bars

Indian spices work well with chocolate as they tend to be strongly perfumed and well balanced and can easily hold their own even in robust, strong chocolates.

**2 tablespoons cumin seeds**

**4 teaspoons coriander seeds**

**14 ounces 66% dark chocolate, tempered**

In a dry frying pan, lightly toast the cumin and coriander seeds over medium heat until they begin to crackle and pop. Grind with a pestle and mortar, then pass through a sieve to remove any unwanted husks. Let cool.

Mix the seeds into the tempered chocolate. Pour the chocolate into your desired chocolate mold. Gently tap or shake the mold to release any air bubbles that may be trapped inside.

Place the chocolate bars in the fridge for no more than 15 minutes to set. To turn the chocolate bars out, invert the mold onto a clean kitchen towel so they don't chip or break. Once the bars are set, wrap in parchment paper and store in a cool, dark place. Eat within a month.

# Wasabi and green apple ganache

This is a strange combination inspired by an amazing cocktail I drank some years ago. The mixologist had infused a whole horseradish in vodka, which he then served in a very chilled shot glass with some green apple liqueur. The flavor was spicy, earthy, fiery, and fruity all at the same time, and I couldn't resist trying to recreate the taste in a chocolate. I use wasabi in place of horseradish, and fresh green apple juice, which adds a deliciously cooling and fruity dimension to the finished chocolate. You can serve the cooled ganache as "shots" as shown in the picture, or use it to fill chocolate shells.

**2 teaspoons wasabi paste, or 1 inch fresh wasabi root, as needed**

**About 6 Granny Smith apples (or a scant 1 cup fresh apple cider)**

**1 cup organic sugar**

**7 ounces fine 66% dark chocolate, chopped**

**1 Granny Smith apple, thinly sliced crosswise, for garnish**

If using fresh wasabi root rather than the paste, you must grate it very finely, then push it through a sieve to extract as much juice out as possible.

Wash the apples, then pass them through a juice extractor, with the skin on; you need about 1 cup.

Put the apple juice, sugar and wasabi paste or pulp in a pan and bring to a simmer. Allow the wasabi to infuse into the apple juice for 5 minutes. Have a taste to test the strength of the wasabi, and add more if desired.

Pour the hot liquid over the chocolate in a heatproof bowl and whisk well until smooth. If you want to use the ganache for cocktails, let the ganache to cool to room temperature and serve in shot glasses, with thin slices of green apple as garnish. Alternatively, refrigerate the ganache and use as a filling for chocolate shells.

# Christmas-pudding truffles

Chocolate naturally lends itself to certain times of year, and especially Christmas. And what could be better than a chocolate that incorporates some of the ingredients most associated with Christmas – cinnamon, dried fruits, orange, Cognac, port, cardamom, and nutmeg, normally found in one essential yuletide dish: Christmas pudding. This truffle has all the flavor of Christmas pud, but without the heavy texture.

**FOR THE GANACHE**

1/3 cup golden raisins

1/3 cup seedless raisins

1 teaspoon ground cinnamon

1/2 teaspoon ground cardamom

1/2 nutmeg, freshly grated

1/3 cup port

2 tablespoons Cognac

Juice and grated zest of 1 orange

3/4 cup heavy cream

2 1/2 cups dark muscovado or brown sugar

18 ounces 70% dark chocolate, chopped

**FOR COATING**

18 ounces 70% dark chocolate, tempered

3 1/2 ounces white chocolate, tempered

Soak the golden raisins, raisins, and spices with the port, Cognac, orange juice and zest for at least 6 hours.

Bring the cream and 2/3 cup water to a simmer, then add the sugar and soaked fruits (with all their liquid) and simmer for 4 minutes. Purée until smooth using an electric blender, then pass through a sieve, pushing as much of the pulp through as possible. Pour over the chocolate in a heatproof bowl and whisk well. Transfer to a plastic container and refrigerate until fully set.

Hand roll the ganache into the desired size. Then, using either your hands or a dipping fork, coat the truffles in tempered dark chocolate, taking care to cover each one fully. Place on parchment paper and let set.

To finish the truffles, carefully spoon a little white chocolate over the top of each truffle to give the look of brandy sauce running down the top and sides.

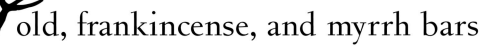

# old, frankincense, and myrrh bars

I love using authentic ingredients to represent the time of year. These Christmas bars are a favorite owing to their unusual flavors but also because they are visually striking with edible gold leaf inlaid into the bars.

**2 leaves of edible gold leaf**

**6 drops of frankincense essential oil**

**8–10 drops of myrrh essential oil**

**18 ounces Venezuelan 70% dark chocolate, tempered**

Prepare your chocolate-bar molds by polishing them with unbleached cotton balls to remove any grease and dust. With clean and dry hands, place a little gold leaf in each bar mold. Avoid sudden movements near the gold leaf or it will fly away.

Mix the essential oils into the tempered chocolate and taste – add more of the oils desired. Spoon the chocolate into the molds and tap sharply five or six times to release any air bubbles trapped in the bottom. Place in the fridge until set and released from the mold; about 10–15 minutes.

Turn out the chocolate onto a clean kitchen towel and wrap in parchment paper or cellophane. Enjoy within 6 months.

*Makes* **40–50 truffles**

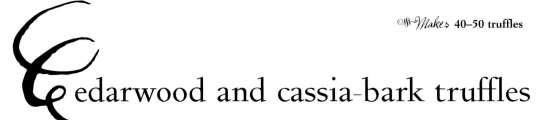

# edarwood and cassia-bark truffles

This is one for the boys with its deeply earthy flavors of cedarwood and cassia bark and dark Venezuelan chocolate. Packed into a box and beautifully wrapped, it makes a stunning and contemporary gift.

**FOR THE GANACHE**

**1 cup heavy cream**

**¾ cup packed light muscovado sugar**

**6 x 3 inch cassia-bark or cinnamon sticks**

**9 ounces Venezuelan 72% dark chocolate, broken into pieces**

**4–6 drops distilled cedarwood essential oil**

**FOR COATING**

**14 ounces Venezuelan 72% dark chocolate, tempered**

**1 cup alkalized cocoa powder**

**2 tablespoons ground cinnamon**

**½ cup confectioners' sugar**

To make the ganache, bring the cream, sugar, and cassia to a boil, then simmer for 2 minutes. Let cool. Add ⅓ cup water and bring back to a boil. Remove from the heat and strain over the chocolate in a heatproof bowl, whisking well. Add the cedarwood oil, mix well, and let cool. Refrigerate for at least 2 hours.

Roll the ganache into even-sized spheres or keep in random-sized, rustic pieces. Sift the cocoa powder, cinnamon and confectioners' sugar together into a wide dish and mix. Dip each truffle into the tempered chocolate, then immediately into the cocoa mixture, and allow to set before removing.

# Herbs & Flowers

I am constantly overwhelmed by the variety and
diversity of herbal and floral flavors at the disposal of
chocolatiers like me – there's no reason for any of us
ever to run out of ideas. Every season has its own herbs
and flowers, but summer is certainly the best time of
year, with florals such as jasmine, bergamot, and
geranium, and herbs such as basil, thyme, and lemon
balm, to name but a few. The most important rule when
you are using these ingredients as your main flavor is
to treat them in a delicate way and never to overcook
them, as this will destroy the aromas and perfumes.
Pure essential oils are perfect for adding an extra
bouquet to your finished chocolate, but make sure
that you use the edible rather than the perfume oils.

# Sweet thyme and jaggery muffins with white chocolate

Early summer, and the first warm mornings arrive with all the anticipation of the long summer days ahead. Relaxing with freshly ground coffee, squeezed fruit juice, and a warm fragrant muffin can be the perfect start to a lazy sunny day. And of course the muffins can help to cheer you up on gloomy rainy days, too.

¾ cup plus 2 tablespoons milk

½ cup grated jaggery (available at Indian grocers) or raw cane sugar

½ cup packed light sugar

Scant ½ cup vegetable oil

2 large organic eggs

⅓ cup thyme leaves

1 teaspoon vanilla extract

2½ cups all-purpose flour

4 teaspoons baking powder

1 teaspoon salt

5½ ounces white chocolate, coarsely chopped

Preheat the oven to 400°F.

In a large bowl, whisk the milk, brown sugar, oil, eggs, thyme leaves, and vanilla.

Whisk together the flour, baking powder, and salt, add to the milk mixture and whisk until just smooth. Stir in the white chocolate.

Line 12 muffin cups with paper liners. Fill each about three-quarters full with the batter. Bake for 20–25 minutes until golden. Let cool and serve warm or store in an airtight container and eat within 5 days.

# Basil and lemon-thyme ganache

When I first began using herbs in my chocolates, I found this combination to be positively musical. Many of our supermarket herbs are grown too quickly and they simply do not have the intense flavor or full character of home-grown ones. Try your local market, as I do, as you will almost certainly find both a better quality and a better price. I use a 66% pure Trinitario bean chocolate from the Caribbean in this recipe, but a delicate fragrant chocolate with 64% or 70% cocoa solids will achieve stunning results also.

**FOR THE GANACHE**

½ cup heavy cream

6 tablespoons organic sugar

⅓ cup packed basil leaves and stalks

3 tablespoons lemon-thyme leaves

12½ ounces Caribbean 66% dark chocolate, chopped

**FOR THE DECORATION**

Juice of 1 lime

½ ounce lemon thyme sprigs

¼ cup organic sugar

17½ ounces Caribbean 66% dark chocolate, tempered

*Paul's top tip*

**Always eat your chocolates at room temperature and never directly from the fridge. Your taste buds cannot identify all the complexities and fragrances of the herbs when they are too cold.**

To make the ganache, place ¾ cup water in a saucepan, along with the cream, sugar, basil, and thyme. Bring to a boil and simmer for 3 minutes, then remove from the heat. Let it cool. Strain and cook again just to the point where the cream begins to simmer.

Strain again over the chocolate in a heatproof bowl and whisk well until smooth and glossy. Taste to check the balance of basil and lemon-thyme flavors. If you think that either flavor is too delicate, then add some more of that herb and allow to infuse in the ganache, then strain it out.

Line a shallow baking dish tray with plastic wrap, letting the excess wrap hang over the sides. Pour in the ganache and let cool, then refrigerate for 1 hour until firm. Lift the ganache out of dish and place on a chopping board, discarding the wrap. Dip a cutter or sharp knife in hot water, dry it off, then cut your desired size and shape.

Alternatively, refrigerate as usual, then roll the ganache into even-sized spheres, using cocoa powder on your fingers to keep the chocolate from melting.

For the decoration, place the lime juice in a saucer, and dip in the sprigs of lemon thyme, coating fully. Shake off any excess juice and sprinkle liberally with sugar. Let dry until crispy and crystallized, then remove the leaves from the stems.

Dip the ganache in the tempered chocolate, then place on plastic sheets or parchment paper. Immediately sprinkle with the crystallized thyme leaves.

Store at room temperature in an airtight container for up to 7 days in a cool dark place, but never the fridge.

# Garden mint ganache

I have a love-hate relationship with minty chocolate as the quality of mint used can vary dramatically. The golden rule when making a ganache is to use fresh mint leaves, since oils and artificial mint flavorings can taste medicinal and have overpowering aftertastes. Not only can you use this ganache to make truffles; while it is soft and silky it can be spread over your favorite cake to create a stunning chocolate mint cake, as shown in the picture opposite.

*Paul's top tip*
Try different varieties such as pineapple mint, spearmint, apple mint, peppermint and my favorite, of course, chocolate mint.

¾ cup fresh mint leaves

½ cup organic sugar

12½ ounces 64% dark chocolate from the Dominican Republic, chopped

Rip the mint leaves roughly to release their natural oils and flavors. Place the sugar in a pan with 1 cup water, bring to a boil and simmer for 3 minutes. Let cool completely. Strain, then bring back to a simmer, pour over the chocolate in a heatproof bowl, and whisk well until smooth. Let cool for around 30 minutes before using.

# Curly parsley, lemon and sea-salt ganache

The inspiration for this unusual chocolate comes from the first salad dressing I ever made – at the age of 13 during a home-economics class. This ganache is fresh and light and perfect for the summer.

⅓ cup fine curly parsley, chopped

Scant 1 cup organic sugar

Juice and zest of 1 lemon

½ teaspoon Maldon sea salt

7 ounces fine 66% dark chocolate, broken into pieces

Put 1¾ cups water in a pan with the chopped parsley, sugar, lemon zest and juice, and salt, bring to a boil and simmer for 2 minutes. Remove from the heat and let stand until cool. Strain, then return to a simmer and pour immediately over the chocolate in a heatproof bowl. Whisk well until the chocolate has fully melted. Allow the ganache to cool. Pipe it into shells, or let it to set in the fridge for hand-rolled truffles.

# Cacao-nib and mint tea tisane

Not being able to find a mint tea that I liked, I decided to experiment with cacao nibs and fresh mint leaves. The result is this heady brew. Cacao nibs are popular in natural food stores and widely available online.

**12 mint leaves**

**1½ teaspoons crushed cacao nibs**

**2 teaspoons palm, light muscovado sugar**

Bring 1¾ cups filtered or mineral water to a boil.

Place 6 mint leaves and the cocoa nibs into each glass, along with a teaspoon of sugar.

Pour on the boiling water and stir until the sugar has dissolved. Wait for the cocoa beans to sink to the bottom of the glass, which takes 2–3 minutes; then it's ready to drink.

In summer, try adding lots of ice for a chilled tisane.

# Thai basil and galangal ganache

Cold infusion (seee page 30) is a great technique for extracting the natural delicate flavors and essential oils from herbs and spices without boiling them, which can reduce the complexities of the ingredients. The shelf life of this ganache is seven days, so it's something to create, make and enjoy while the flavors last.

*Paul's top tip*
**When making cold infusions, wash the ingredients first to remove any dirt. Note that you need to use more of the herb or spice than you would normally, as the flavor will be delicate and light.**

**⅔ cup Thai basil leaves, roughly torn**

**1 x 2-inch piece galangal or ginger, peeled and grated**

**1½ cups organic sugar**

**10½ ounces Madagascan 64% dark chocolate, chopped**

Put the basil and grated galangal into a saucepan. Add a scant 1 cup water and infuse for 6 to 8 hours in a cool place.

Add the sugar to the infused liquid and warm to 140°F, until the sugar is fully dissolved. Remove from the heat, add the chocolate and blend well using an electric hand blender. Strain out the galangal and basil. Let the ganache cool for 30 minutes before using to fill shells; or refrigerate until set to make hand-rolled truffles.

# *L*emon-thyme caramel

Lemon thyme isn't the most obvious herb to pair with caramel, but its delicate floral fragrance and vibrant citrus taste balance perfectly with the slightly salty caramel. Not only is it perfect for making a filled chocolate, but also the caramel is delicious served warm over ice cream or shaken into a classic martini.

**11 tablespoons unsalted butter**

**¾ cup packed light muscovado sugar**

**⅔ cup lemon-thyme leaves**

**1 tablespoon fine sea salt**

**½ cup heavy cream**

**2 ounces finest-quality milk chocolate, finely chopped**

Melt the butter in a large saucepan, add the sugar and stir until dissolved. Add the thyme leaves, bring to a boil and simmer for 5 minutes. Add the salt and mix until dissolved.

Remove the pan from the heat and add the cream, standing back as it can splutter at this stage. Whisk well until all the cream is incorporated. Add the milk chocolate and whisk until fully melted. Strain through a very fine sieve to remove the thyme leaves. Let cool.

Store for up to 2 months in the fridge in airtight jars.

*Paul's top tip*
Never use rock salt when making caramel, as it won't dissolve fully and you will be left with very hard crunchy salt crystals in your otherwise lovely and smooth caramel.

# *C*hile and crystallized lemongrass ganache

In this recipe I have used Thai ingredients to create a vibrant and colorful ganache. As an alternative to making chocolates, you can use the ganache as a scrumptiously rich chocolate pudding.

**FOR THE GANACHE**

**2 stalks lemongrass**

**1½ cups organic sugar**

**1 fresh red chile, seeded and minced, and chopped finely**

**1½ pounds white chocolate, chopped**

**FOR COATING**

**About 10½ ounces fine 66% dark chocolate, tempered**

To make the ganache, remove all the woody outer leaves from the lemongrass and chop very finely.

Put 1¼ cups water in a pan with the sugar and bring to a simmer. Add the lemongrass and chile and simmer for 15 minutes until soft. Pour over the white chocolate in a bowl and whisk until smooth. Refrigerate until set.

Roll the ganache into even-sized spheres, then dip into the tempered chocolate. Alternatively, pour the warm ganache into small coffee cups and allow to cool. Refrigerate and serve with sugar cookies or tropical fruits such as lychee and mango.

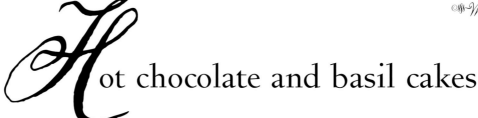 

# Hot chocolate and basil cakes

The first chocolate molten cakes I ever made was while I was head pastry chef for Marco Pierre White, and the moment I tasted it I knew this was going to become a classic dessert. These days, you can even find cake mixes for these little cakes with gooey centers. This recipe has a filling of creamy, delicately infused white chocolate with flecks of fragrant basil. The color and flavor contrast makes this a perfect dinner-party dessert.

### FOR THE FILLING

⅓ cup heavy cream

⅓ cup packed basil leaves

7 ounces white chocolate, chopped

### FOR THE CAKES

6 tablespoons unsalted butter

3 ounces Caribbean 66% dark chocolate, chopped

3 large organic eggs

6 tablespoons organic sugar

½ cup all-purpose flour

### FOR THE MOLDS

2 tablespoons unsalted butter, melted

¼ cup all-purpose flour, for dusting

Start by making the ganache filling, as it must be set before it can be used. Bring the cream and basil to a simmer. Remove from the heat and use a hand blender to break the basil leaves into small pieces. Pour over the white chocolate in a heatproof bowl and whisk well. Pour into a plastic container and refrigerate for at least an hour until set. Once set, make 4 balls of the ganache and refrigerate until needed.

For the cakes, melt the butter carefully over low heat. Remove from the heat, add the dark chocolate, and mix well. Whisk the eggs and sugar together lightly and whisk into the chocolate mixture, whisking well. Add the flour and stir well until smooth.

Prepare 4 dariole molds or ramekins by brushing each one with melted butter and then dusting with flour. Fill each one-third full with the batter, then refrigerate for 30 minutes.

Remove from the fridge, place a ball of basil ganache in each mold and fill up with the remaining chocolate batter. Refrigerate for 1 hour before baking.

To cook, first preheat the oven to 350°F. Place the molds on a baking tray for 9 minutes. Do not open the oven until the full bakin gtime has passed.

To serve, using a thick paper towel, carefully invert each cake onto a dessert plate and lift off the mold. Serve immediately with ice cream or cold crème fraîche.

# Rosemary and pear truffles

Autumn is such a comforting season with its crisp days, golden colors and warming flavors. And it brings with it many delicious fruits such as apples, plums, blackberries, elderberries, quince, and, of course, pears – all of which work wonderfully in chocolate desserts and truffles. Comice pears are beautifully soft and intensely fragrant when ripe, so they blend well into a smooth truffle mixture, while rosemary adds a woody and fresh taste to the ganache. These truffles are perfect eaten with warming whisky, rich sherry or a robust red wine.

**6 Comice pears**

**1 ⅓ cups packed light muscovado sugar**

**⅓ cup heavy cream**

**¼ cup sprigs of rosemary, leaves stripped from the stalk**

**9 ounces Caribbean 66% dark chocolate, broken into pieces**

**About 10½ ounces dark chocolate, tempered**

Preheat the oven to 350°F.

Peel and halve the pears, then remove the cores. Place in a baking dish, cover with foil and bake for about 30 minutes or until very soft.

Bring the sugar, ⅔ cup water, the cream, and rosemary to a boil then simmer for 2 minutes. Remove from the heat and process in a blender with the pears until very smooth. Pass the mixture through a sieve, pushing the flesh of the pear through with the back of a spatula or wooden spoon.

Add the 9 ounces chocolate and whisk well until glossy. The pear flesh gives the ganache a slightly grainy texture. Allow the ganache to cool, then refrigerate until fully set.

Scoop generous teaspoonfuls of ganache onto a baking tray and coat with your favorite tempered dark chocolate.

# Saffron and Greek thyme honey ganache

In my opinion, saffron is one of the most complex and interesting spices, especially when blended with chocolate. It can be quite difficult to pair chocolate with so fragrant and intoxicating a spice, the challenge being to find a delicate chocolate that enhances and complements the saffron rather than overpowers it. I have chosen to use Greek thyme honey as the sweetener since its heady perfume and rich flavor balance perfectly with saffron.

**FOR THE GANACHE**

**3 tablespoons Greek thyme honey**

**1 teaspoon saffron threads**

**14 ounces white chocolate, chopped**

**12 ounces 64–68% dark chocolate or white chocolate, tempered**

**FOR THE DECORATION**

**Edible gold powder (optional)**

Bring a scant 1 cup water, the honey and the saffron to a simmer in a pan, then remove from the heat and infuse for 15 minutes. Bring the liquid back to a simmer. Remove from the heat then add the white chocolate and whisk well until smooth. The saffron threads should be visible in the ganache and will continue to release their vibrant egg-yolk-yellow color.

The ganache can be used in either white or dark chocolate shells. I like to create a rectangular shell to create a thinner chocolate that melts in the mouth more quickly. My advice when using dark shells is to use a fragrant chocolate of 64–68% cocoa solids from either Venezuela or the Caribbean. I use Valrhona 66% Caraibe as the delicate finish of the chocolate never drowns the glorious saffron. Brush each chocolate with edible gold powder, if using, to add a touch of luxury.

Alternatively, try pouring the ganache into small dessert cups or dessert wineglasses, then leave to cool and enjoy with a clean sable cookies or with fresh delicate fruits such as apricots, figs or dates. Refrigerate if not to be eaten straight away.

Troy descrip of, and the Plain of

Travellers, tales for

# Alcohol

I am huge fan of chocolate and alcohol as a combination. I have my mum to thank for this, as she used to give me a box of Famous Names liqueur chocolates every Christmas. I absolutely loved them and felt ever so sophisticated when eating all the different fillings of brandy, sherry, whisky, and coffee liqueur. The warming feeling of the liqueur at the back of the throat mingled with the strong dark chocolate is a marriage made in chocolate heaven.

The following recipes will give you the confidence to use alcohol and chocolate together without the risk of overpowering the flavors of either. As there are so many varieties of alcohol and characteristics within, when experimenting be sure to blend a little of the alcohol and the chocolate in the mouth at the same time.

# The ultimate chocolate martini

There are many versions of a chocolate martini, but how many are made with real chocolate? Most use flavored syrups or liqueurs to add the chocolate flavor, but I believe that only real chocolate keeps the martini's clean crisp taste; and if you like your martini extra dry, then the chocolate does not detract.

**FOR THE CHOCOLATE LIQUOR**

**3½ ounces 70% dark chocolate, chopped**

**½ cup organic sugar**

**FOR THE COCKTAIL**

**Crushed ice**

**4 ounces gin or vodka**

**2 ounces dry vermouth (Noilly Prat is my preference)**

**Cocoa powder, for dusting**

To make the chocolate liquor, put ½ cup water, the chocolate and sugar in a saucepan and bring to a simmer over a low heat, stirring constantly. Remove from the heat and let cool.

Chill 2 large martini glasses in the freezer for 1 hour.

Half-fill a cocktail shaker with crushed ice, then add four ¼ cup measures of the chocolate liquor with the gin and vermouth. Shake well. Strain into the frozen glasses, dust the top with cocoa powder, and serve.

# Pimm's cocktail truffles

I dream of long, balmy summer evenings with a large pitcher of ice-cold Pimm's garnished with cucumber, strawberries, and mint to share with friends. This fresh and light truffle is made for such an occasion, and is best served slightly chilled (five minutes will do) for a cooling and tingling chocolate experience.

½ cup granulated sugar

½ cup cucumber, peeled, seeded, and diced

8 large strawberries, hulled

⅓ cup mint leaves

1 ¼ pounds Caribbean 66% dark chocolate, broken into pieces

⅔ cup Pimm's

Bring $1\frac{1}{3}$ cups water to a simmer with the sugar, chopped cucumber, strawberries and mint. Cook for 5 minutes, then blend until smooth. Pour into a cheesecloth-lined sieve over a bowl and drain overnight until only the pulp is left.

Bring the liquid back to a simmer, then pour over the chocolate in a heatproof bowl, whisking well until smooth. Now add the Pimm's, and whisk until fully incorporated. Cool for 30 minutes and pipe into shells, or refrigerate until set and roll into truffles once set.

# Absinthe and peppermint truffles

I love creating daring combinations that become a hot topic for discussion at the dinner table. Take great care in buying your absinthe, as there are some poor-quality varieties available without the unique wormwood and herbal flavors: always look for a "deluxe" version, and choose a reputable brand.

½ cup organic sugar

9 ounces Caribbean 66% dark chocolate, chopped

⅓ cup absinthe deluxe

3 drops peppermint essential oil

About 30 dark chocolate shells and 10½ ounces dark chocolate, tempered

Bring $\frac{2}{3}$ cup water to a simmer in a pan, then add the sugar and stir until dissolved. Remove from the heat. Add the chocolate and whisk well until smooth. Let cool.

Gradually mix the absinthe into the ganache, tasting after each addition to check the strength of flavor. Next, add the peppermint oil and mix well.

Let cool for 30 minutes before filling and closing the chocolate shells. Enjoy within 4 weeks of making.

# Apple cider punch truffles

**Autumn flavors inspire me more than those of any other season. I can't get enough of the fruits which have been hanging on for dear life all summer, soaking up the sun, becoming sweeter and more fragrant by the day, and eventually becoming ripe, ready for harvesting and eating. Unfortunately, most fruit you buy in the supermarket simply does not have the texture, flavor, or appearance of a true orchard fruit. Locally-grown apples are much more likely to be deliciously crisp and fragrant. This recipe makes a lot of truffles, so is ideal for when you want to make a big enough batch to give away or to share. You could put the chocolates in gift bags and give them to your friends for Christmas, or serve a big pile of them at a party.**

**FOR THE GANACHE**

**1 3/4 cups hard apple cider (Heron Valley is particularly good)**

**1 cup light muscovado brown sugar**

**1 cinnamon stick, broken in half**

**5 cloves**

**4 star anise, crushed**

**2 green cardamom pods, crushed**

**1/2 nutmeg, freshly grated**

**1 1/2 pounds Madagascan 50% milk chocolate, chopped**

**FOR COATING**

**14 ounces Madagascan 64% dark chocolate, tempered**

**1 3/4 cups alkalized cocoa powder**

Bring 1 cup of the cider to a simmer with all the sugar and spices. Turn off the heat and infuse for 15 minutes. Strain out the spices and pour the liquid into a heatproof bowl set over gently simmering water. Add the chocolate and stir until you have a thick glossy ganache.

Remove from the heat and whisk in the remaining cider. The addition of cold cider will help preserve the ganache as the alcohol will not have been cooked off. Cool the ganache, then pour into a large shallow dish and refrigerate until fully set.

To coat, begin by scooping uneven-sized pieces of ganache (taking little care about size or shape) and place onto a tray covered with parchment paper. Prepare a bowl of tempered chocolate and large baking sheet with the cocoa powder.

Drop the ganache into the tempered chocolate, coating fully, then lift out with a dipping fork, tapping to allow any excess chocolate to drop back. Immediately drop the truffle into the tray of cocoa powder and allow to set, the idea being that the truffles have one glossy chocolate side and a cocoa side. Shake to remove any excess cocoa powder.

Pour a glass of hot mulled cider and serve the truffles alongside.

# Traditional-ale truffles

The first time I combined real ale with chocolate was my first Christmas at my chocolaterie, when I needed something traditional and ended up using rich, malty London Ale. I experimented with many different chocolates, and concluded that the winning variety was Valrhona's Jivara Lait 40% milk chocolate (from Java); its malt extract and intensely creamy finish pairs perfectly with the bittersweet ale. You can choose any ale you like, but do taste it first for bitterness; you may then need to increase or decrease the sugar level in the recipe.

**1 cup ale**

**½ cup packed light muscovado sugar**

**1 pound Javanese 40% milk chocolate, chopped**

**14 ounces 70% dark chocolate, tempered**

Put ¼ cup of the ale and the sugar in a saucepan and stir over low heat until the sugar is fully dissolved. Add the remaining ale and warm until you can see the alcohol's vapors being released from the surface. The ale needs only to be warm enough to melt the chocolate – overheating it will cook off the alcohol which is the natural preservative in this ganache.

Pour the ale into a blender and add the chocolate gradually on medium speed until smooth. Cool for 30 minutes and pipe into shells, or leave to set in the fridge, then hand roll into truffles. Use the tempered chocolate for coating.

A simple decoration of piped milk chocolate looks good on these truffles but is optional.

# Chocolate bramble cocktail

I came up with this version of the classic bramble cocktail one evening when the air in the city changed from warm and balmy to the first cool breeze of autumn.

**FOR THE CHOCOLATE LIQUOR**

2¾ cups organic sugar

5½ ounces 70% dark chocolate, chopped

**FOR THE REST**

Juice of ½ lemon

⅓ cup gin (I prefer Tanqueray or Plymouth Dry)

5 teaspoons Crème de Mûres (blackberry liqueur)

8 blackberries

Lots of crushed ice

2 thin squares of your favorite dark chocolate

First, make the chocolate liquor. Put ½ cup water in a saucepan along with the sugar and bring to a simmer. Let rest for 2 minutes, then pour over the chocolate pieces in a heatproof bowl. Whisk well and let cool thoroughly.

Meanwhile, chill 2 martini glasses in the freezer for at least 30 minutes to get the frosted effect.

In a cocktail shaker or pitcher, place gin, the lemon juice, Crème de Mûres and 6 of the blackberries. Muddle and mix well until the blackberries burst slightly.

Place a pyramid of crushed ice into each glass and pour over the blackberry mixture. Now top up each glass with the chocolate liquor, then place a blackberry and a piece of dark chocolate on top of each ice pyramid.

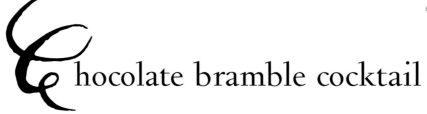

# Glenmorangie Quinta Ruban caramel

Glenmorangie Quinta Ruban (extra matured in port casks) has particular sparkle and shine. The rose-hued Scotch has complex, aromatic flavors which work wonderfully in this rich caramel. Perfect in autumn and winter, the caramel is stunning warmed and poured over ice cream, meringues, and other desserts.

7 tablespoons unsalted butter

½ cup packed light muscovado sugar

2 teaspoons sea salt

⅓ cup heavy cream

9 ounces Madagascan 50% milk chocolate, chopped

¼ cup Glenmorangie Quinta Ruban Scotch whisky

Melt the butter in a large saucepan, then add the sugar and salt and boil for 4 minutes. Remove from the heat, add the heavy cream and whisk. Add the chocolate and mix well. Allow to cool, then add the whisky.

# Hendrick's gin, cucumber and rose ganache

There is something really quite special about gin, because there are so many different varieties which all taste completely different from one another. Some are very botanical, some are heavy with juniper berry, and some are fragrant and intoxicating. Hendrick's gin is infused with cucumber and rose, and this ganache can be used to make a dipping fondue, or cocktails for summer, or simply used to fill chocolate shells.

**1 cup organic sugar**

**4 ounces English (seedless) cucumber, diced**

**⅓ cup Hendrick's gin**

**¾ pound fine 66% dark chocolate, chopped**

**4–6 drops rose essential oil**

Bring 1 cup water to a simmer with the sugar and cucumber, then pour into a blender and purée. Pass through a fine sieve and pour back into the saucepan. Add the gin and heat gently until warm enough to melt the chocolate, but do not allow to simmer. Pour over the chocolate in a bowl and whisk well. Add the rose oil and whisk again.

If serving as a fondue (as shown left), pour the ganache into a serving bowl while still warm and serve with pieces of brownie and delicate fruits like strawberries, peaches and nectarines. Alternatively, allow the ganache to cool to room temperature and shake it with vermouth and more Hendrick's gin for a stunning summer martini. If you want to make truffles, this ganache is best cooled and piped into shells.

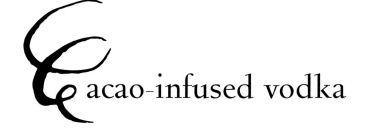

# Cacao-infused vodka

This is probably the simplest recipe in my book yet definitely one of the most gorgeous. Once the vodka is ready, it is perfect to use in either desserts or cocktails. You must be prepared to nurture the vodka for one month to help the infusion, but it is well worth the wait.

**one 1-quart bottle of premium vodka (my preference is Grey Goose)**

**7 ounces cacao nibs**

Pour about 1 cup of the vodka out of the bottle and save for another use. I suggest using the extra vodka for chocolate martinis (see page 108).

Pour the cocoa nibs through a funnel into the bottle, close, and shake well. Then simply shake every day for one month, then leave for one week more to settle. Enjoy as required.

# Mulled-wine hot chocolate

It was inevitable that at some point I would come up with this recipe as I love both mulled wine and hot chocolate. A warming, indulgent and very boozy drink, it is definitely one for adults only.

**2 cups organic sugar**

**2 cups alkalized cocoa powder**

**2 cinnamon sticks**

**5 star anise**

**8 cloves**

**18 ounces 67% dark chocolate from the Dominican Republic, broken into pieces**

**2 clementines or satsumas, skin left on, halved**

**1 sprig of fresh rosemary**

**1 x 750ml bottle of fruity red wine, such as Merlot**

Put 1³/4 cups water, the sugar, the cocoa powder and all the spices in a saucepan and bring to a simmer. Remove from the heat, add the chocolate, and whisk well until the chocolate is fully incorporated. Add the clementines and rosemary and infuse for 10 minutes. Add the red wine and warm through gently.

Serve warm rather than hot.

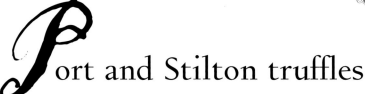

# Port and Stilton truffles

This truffle has become a permanent fixture in my House Collection, and I created it to appeal mainly to my male customers who were looking for something robust, masculine and heavier in texture.

**¾ cup heavy cream**

**6 tablespoons organic sugar**

**4 ounces very mature Stilton cheese, roughly chopped**

**18 ounces 70% dark chocolate, broken into pieces**

**¼ cup tawny port**

Put ³/4 cup water, the cream, sugar and cheese in a saucepan and bring to a simmer. Pour over the chocolate in a heatproof bowl and whisk well until smooth. Add the port, mixing well until incorporated. Cool and use to fill chocolate shells or leave to set in the fridge for hand-rolled truffles.

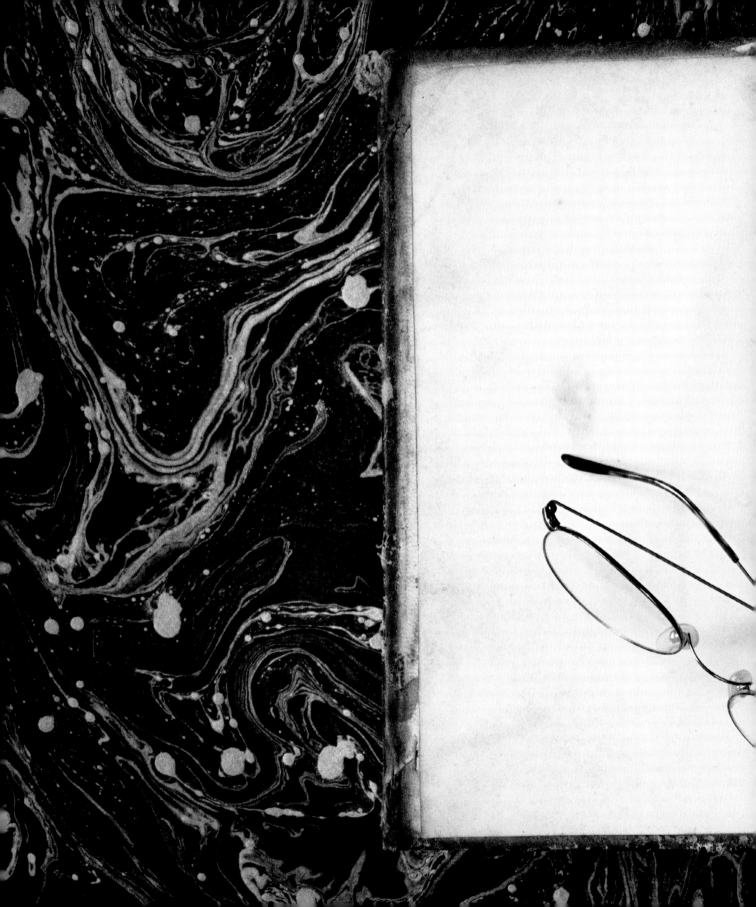

# *Alchemy*

Experimentation is the most exciting time for the chocolatier as it allows one's creative thinking to go wild. For me, the experiments really took off with my Marmite ganache back in 2006, when I was challenged to make this unusual combination work. I am still selling Marmite truffles three years on. While it is a chocolate to love or hate, the Marmite truffle has enabled me to launch some very creative and experimental combinations without their having the gimmick tag associated with these mad-scientist-style chocolates. I hope this chapter inspires you to try something new and helps to build your confidence when you are working with chocolate.

# Paul's Venezuelan chocolate chile chicken

There are very many versions of chocolate chile chicken, but I chose to include this one as it's fantastically quick and easy to make. I can't promise it's authentic, but it does have the wow factor, and the Venezuelan chocolate adds a deep rich glossy finish and flavor.

4 organic chicken thighs

4 organic chicken drumsticks

1 tablespoon olive oil

4 large shallots, finely chopped

2 garlic cloves, finely chopped

Juice and zest of 3 oranges

14½ ounce can tomatoes, chopped

3 fresh red chiles, seeded and minced

2 teaspoons dried pure ground ancho chile (or any other mild chiles, ground in a spice grinder)

1 tablespoon coriander seeds

1 tablespoon dark muscovado sugar

5½ ounces Venezuelan dark chocolate, chopped

⅓ cup coarsely torn cilantro leaves

Preheat the oven to 400°F.

In a casserole dish over medium high heat, brown the chicken pieces in batches, and put on a plate. Add the shallots and garlic and stir until softened, about 1 minute. Pour in the orange juice and zest and stir up the browned bits in the casserole. Add the tomatoes with their juices, fresh and dried chiles, coriander seeds, and sugar, bring to a boil, then simmer for 5 minutes. Cover with the lid and bake for 20 minutes.

Remove from the oven, lift out the chicken and stir the chocolate into the remaining sauce. Return the chicken to the casserole, sprinkle with the cilantro and serve with the sauce smothered over the chicken.

# Savory sauces for meat, fish and vegetables

Savory sauces using chocolate and cocoa beans have long been popular in Mexican culture, with recipes dating back centuries; the best-known example is mole (pronounced mol-ay), a complex spice blend including nutmeg, cinnamon, and chile, most commonly served with chicken. I decided to create three new sauces, one each for white meat, fish, and red meat and vegetables. They are all very different from one another, with different textures and flavors. All can be easily prepared and made in advance and stored in the fridge until needed.

*Makes* about 1¹/₃ cups

# Chocolate sauce for white meat

**8 shallots, finely chopped**

**1 tablespoon extra virgin olive oil**

**1 teaspoon fine sea salt**

**¹/₃ cup dry sherry or dry white wine**

**1³/₄ cups chicken stock**

**³/₄ cup heavy cream**

**Freshly ground white pepper**

**3¹/₂ ounces Caribbean 66% dark chocolate, or other delicate fragrant chocolate, chopped**

**Tender herb of your choice, such as sage, cilantro, parsley, tarragon, or sorrel**

Sweat the shallots in the olive oil and salt in a covered saucepan over low heat, until soft. Deglaze the saucepan with the sherry and simmer to reduce by two-thirds. Pour in the chicken stock and reduce again by two-thirds. Add the heavy cream, and salt and pepper to taste, and simmer for 1 minute.

Pour over the hot liquid over the chocolate in a heatproof bowl, whisking well until smooth. Chop the herbs, then stir into the sauce. Serve immediately, or place in a plastic container, cool, and refrigerate until needed. Reheat gently before using.

# White Chocolate sauce for seafood

5 shallots, finely chopped

1 tablespoon olive oil

¾ cup fish stock

½ cup crème fraîche

Juice and zest of ½ lemon

7 ounces white chocolate, chopped

3 tablespoons anise liqueur, such as Pernod or Ouzo

3 tablespoons finely chopped fresh parsley

3 tablespoons finely chopped fresh dill

Sea salt and freshly ground white pepper

Sweat the shallots gently in the olive oil until soft. Add the stock and simmer to reduce by two-thirds. Add the crème fraîche and lemon juice and zest simmer for 5 minutes. Pour over the white chocolate in a bowl, whisking well until smooth and glossy. Add the alcohol, parsley, dill, and salt and pepper to taste.

Serve immediately or place in a plastic container, cool, and refrigerate until needed. Reheat gently before serving.

# Chocolate sauce for red meat and vegetables

5 shallots, finely chopped

1 tablespoon light olive oil

2 tablespoons tomato paste

Spices, such as chile, cinnamon or nutmeg (optional)

²/₃ cup robust red wine, or port

2 tablespoons light muscovado sugar

Scant 1 cup beef or vegetable stock

¼ teaspoon fine sea salt

Black pepper, to taste

Herbs, e.g. rosemary, thyme, sage, parsley or bay leaves (optional)

2 ounces African 85% dark chocolate, chopped

Sweat the shallots gently in the olive oil in a covred saucepan over low heat until soft. Add the tomato paste and cook for 1 minute; if using spices in your sauce, add them now.

Add the red wine and sugar and simmer to reduce by two-thirds. Now add the stock, salt and pepper, and any herbs you might be using (chopped well first). Simmer to reduce until the sauce is reduced by about half; this can take up to 30 minutes.

Pour the hot liquid over the chocolate in a heatproof bowl, whisking well. Serve place in a plastic container, cool, and refrigerate until needed. Reheat gently before serving.

# Honey-cured bacon, Stilton and chocolate sandwich

My favorite brunch sandwich is a combination of honey-cured bacon, rich dark chocolate, and ripe tangy Stilton. Mouthwatering and satisfying.

**4 thick slices of hand-cut, crusty white bread**

**Soft salted butter, for spreading**

**2 ounces Venezuelan 72% dark chocolate**

**6 slices honey-cured bacon**

**3 ounces very ripe Stilton**

Preheat the boiler until very hot. Lightly toast the bread on both sides, then spread with butter. Grate the chocolate on top and return to the boiler briefly to melt, taking care not to let the chocolate burn. Remove. Immediately grill the bacon until the edges are crisp and caramelized. Place on the chocolate and finish with a generous crumbling of Stilton. Lay the remaining buttered slice on top and press firmly. Enjoy!

# Savory sandwich ganache

At this point, you may think I am pushing the boundaries too far, but I can assure you that this savory ganache is wonderfully delicious and versatile.

**4 ounces cream cheese**

**2 tablespoons light muscovado sugar**

**1 tablespoon Worcestershire sauce**

**1 teaspoon fine sea salt**

**9 ounces African 85% dark chocolate**

**3 tablespoons extra virgin olive oil**

Bring 3 tablespoons water, the cream cheese, sugar, Worcestershire sauce, and salt to a simmer for 2 minutes. Pour the hot liquid over the chocolate in a heatproof bowl, whisking well until smooth. Cool for 30 minutes. Whisk in the olive oil until emulsified. Pour into sterilized jars and use within one week, or refrigerate and use within a month.

I'm sure you'll be able to come up with your own ideas for using this ganache in sandwiches, but here are some tried and tested combinations: Stilton, bacon and chicken; Stilton and pear (great toasted); chicken and wild mushroom; arugula and Gorgonzola; and cream cheese and smoked chicken. Experiment and enjoy!

# Jerusalem artichoke soup with chocolate pecorino wafers

Earthy flavors marry well with Venezuelan chocolate. This recipe brings together deeply earthy Jerusalem artichokes with tangy pecorino cheese and lots of Venezuelan chocolate to balance and blend the flavors.

### FOR THE VELOUTÉ

1 tablespoon olive oil

1 pound Jerusalem artichokes, washed and diced

1 onion, diced

1 leek, white part only, thinly sliced

Handful of celery leaves, chopped

2 garlic cloves, chopped

2 teaspoons fine sea salt

14 ounces freshly ground black pepper

1 small baking potato, peeled and diced

4²⁄₃ cups vegetable stock

3 ounces white chocolate

½ cup heavy cream

1 tablespoon fresh thyme leaves

### FOR THE WAFERS

1 cup (4 ounces) pecorino Romano, finely grated

2½ tablespoons cacao nibs, coarsely chopped

4 ounces Venezuelan 72% dark chocolate, chopped

To make the soup, heat the oil in a large saucepan, then add the Jerusalem artichokes, onion, leek, celery leaves, garlic, and salt and pepper. Sweat, with the lid on, over very low heat for 10 minutes, until soft. Add the hot stock and potato and cook for 20 minutes.

Blend the mixture well until very smooth. Strain though a sieve to remove any fibers and pour into a clean saucepan. Stir in the white chocolate, cream and thyme leaves. (The soup can be kept at room temperature for up to 2 hours.)

To make the wafers, line a baking sheet with parchment paper or a silicone mat (which has good nonstick qualities). Preheat the oven to 350°F.

Mix the pecorino with the cocoa nibs. Sprinkle a tablespoon of the mixture onto parchment paper and shape into a triangle or disc shape using an icing spatula. Repeat for the rest of the mixture.

Bake the pecorino wafers for 6–8 minutes, until golden. Allow them to cool fully, then carefully lift off the paper with the spatula.

Melt the chocolate in a hot water bath using the icing spatula or pastry brush, coat the underside of each wafer with chocolate, then place back onto the parchment paper, chocolate side up, and let set.

Serve the soup hot or it will curdle with the wafers passed alongside for your guests to dip or stir in the soup.

# Wild mushroom ganache

This unusual ganache is ideal for both savory dishes and sweet truffles, as its delicate, earthy flavors can be paired well with many different ingredients, especially autumnal and wintry flavors. Serve it warm with savory dishes such as fresh asparagus, or roast partridge or pheasant, or allow to cool and use to fill your chosen chocolate shells for an interesting truffle.

²/₃ cup heavy cream

½ cup packed light muscovado sugar

4 teaspoons dried porcini powder, or ¾ ounce dried porcini mushrooms, ground in a spice grinder

1 teaspoon Maldon sea salt

10½ ounces Ghanaian 68% dark chocolate, chopped

Bring ²/₃ cup water, the cream, sugar, porcini powder, and salt or mushrooms to the boil and simmer for 3 minutes. Pour into a blender and purée for 30 seconds, then strain through a fine sieve.

Return to the saucepan and bring back to a simmer, then pour over the chocolate in a heatproof bowl and whisk well until smooth. Use as desired.

# Sweet chocolate pesto

I love having jars of deliciously flavorsome jams, spreads, preserves, and pickles in my cupboard, especially when they are homemade. This pesto is totally different and fantastic for light summer pasta, rice and roasted-vegetable salads, and is also great simply spread on white-fleshed fish and baked. The recipe is very simple and quick to prepare.

½ cup fresh basil leaves

½ cup extra virgin olive oil

Juice and zest of ½ lemon

½ teaspoon fine sea salt

½ cup (2 ounces) pine nuts

1 cup (4 ounces) pecorino cheese, grated

1 ounce Venezuelan 100% dark chocolate, grated

Place all the ingredients into a small blender – or use a mortar and pestle – and blend until you reach your preferred texture – chunky or smooth, or somewhere in between. Spoon the pesto into a sterilized jar or jars, seal, and keep airtight.

Stored in a sealed jar, the pesto will keep in the fridge for a month. Once open, use within 1–2 weeks. Cover the top of any remaining pesto with a thin layer of olive oil.

# Plum tomato ganache

Save this recipe for when a summertime trip to your local farmer's market yields the sweetest, juciest plum (Roma) tomatoes. Try piping the ganache into shells and serving as an unusual *amuse-bouche* before a meal.

18 ounces ripe plum (Roma) tomatoes

½ cup organic sugar

1 teaspoon fine sea salt

18 ounces 66% dark chocolate, chopped

Bring a saucepan of water to a simmer and plunge in the tomatoes for 30 seconds. Refresh them immediately in iced water, then remove the skins. Place the tomatoes in a blender and purée into a smooth paste is formed. Place the pulp into a double layer of cheese cloth, tie it tightly at the top and hang over a mixing bowl for 24 hours.

Squeeze the final droplets of tomato juices from the cloth and discard the cloth and its contents. You should have 1⅓ cups – add water if needed. Pour into a saucepan with the sugar and salt and bring to simmer (do not boil). Pour over the chocolate in a heatproof bowl and whisk well. Allow to cool thoroughly before using.

# Salted black-olive bars

Black olives in a chocolate bar? Yes indeed, and they work beautifully when semi-dried in slithers thoughout the chocolate. Choose sun-dried olives not in oil, brine, or marinade and make sure they have not been artificially ripened with the use of chemicals. The more you pay, the better the olive in most cases.

7 ounces sun-dried black olives, pitted and cut into slivers lengthwise

½ teaspoon fine sea salt

1¼ pounds Ghanaian 68% dark chocolate, tempered

Preheat the oven to 225°F. Lay the olive slivers on some parchment paper on a baking sheet and bake for 2 hours until semi-dried. The texture should be dry but not crisp or too chewy.

Stir the olives into the chocolate with the salt, and pour into the desired molds to set.

The bars should be eaten within a month.

# Dark chocolate and chile gnocchi, with mascarpone and pecorino

Gnocchi are one of my top comfort foods, so I just had to share this recipe with you. The secret to creating the perfectly light little dumpling is getting the correct balance of potato, flour and egg in the gnocchi dough. You won't be surprised to hear that I have added some cocoa powder to the flour, which adds a deep flavor – not too chocolatey, but enough to stand up against the chile and pecorino.

## FOR THE GNOCCHI

**6 tablespoons all-purpose flour**

**3 tablespoons alkalized cocoa powder**

**½ teaspoon chile powder (choose your preferred heat level: ancho, cayenne, or habanero)**

**Pinch of sea salt**

**1½ ounces baking potato, boiled and mashed**

**1 large organic egg yolk**

**1 tablespoon extra virgin olive oil**

## TO SERVE

**7 ounces mascarpone, at room temperature**

**Freshly ground black pepper**

**3 tablespoons fresh oregano leaves**

**½ cup (2 ounces) freshly grated pecorino Romano**

In a large mixing bowl or in a food mixer on low speed, combine together the mashed potatoes, flour, cocoa, chile powder, and salt. Add the yolk and knead to form a smooth dough; if you are using a food mixer, then use the dough-hook attachment for this stage. Wrap the dough in plastic wrap and rest in the refrigerator for 1 hour.

To shape the gnocchi, cut the dough into half. Roll one portion into a long sausage shape, sprinkling flour on the surface if the dough gets sticky. Cut the dough into even-sized pieces roughly 1 inch long. You can leave the gnocchi this shape or, to give an attractive finish, roll the back of a fork over each little dumpling to give a lined pattern and rounded shape. Place the gnocchi on a plate covered with plastic wrap until you're ready to cook them, within 2 hours.

Bring a large pot of salted water to a simmer over high heat. Add in the gnocchi and cook until they float to the surface. Once they're floating, remove from the water with a slotted spoon to kitchen towels to drain.

Heat the olive oil in a large frying pan over a medium heat and cook the gnocchi on each side. They should look golden and be springy to the touch. Remove from the pan and keep warm.

Season the mascarpone with black pepper and mix well. To serve, place the gnocchi on a warm plate with small spoonfuls of the mascarpone, and grated cheese and oregano sprinkled over the top.

# 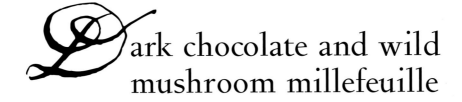ark chocolate and wild mushroom millefeuille

This hearty main course shows that you don't have to compromise with the absence of meat. It is filling, packed with flavor and full of different textures. The addition of African 85% dark chocolate balances the heady earthy mushroom flavors and adds a savory taste sometimes lacking in vegetarian dishes.

**14 ounces store-bought puff pastry**

**1 large organic egg yolk, beaten for glazing**

**1 tablespoon olive oil**

**2 shallots, thinly sliced**

**3 garlic cloves, thinly sliced**

**1 tablespoon finely chopped rosemary leaves**

**4 ounces oyster mushrooms**

**3 ounces cremini mushrooms**

**2 ounces chanterelles**

**2 ounces fresh porcini or shiitake cups**

**3 tablespoons Madeira**

**1 teaspoon fine sea salt**

**½ teaspoon freshly ground white pepper**

**¾ cup heavy cream**

**3 ounces African 85% dark chocolate, broken into pieces**

**About 25 chives, cut into 2-inch pieces**

**Extra virgin olive oil, for serving**

Roll out the puff pastry to ¼ inch thick, then cut into two rectangles: 3 x 5 inch for main-course size, or 2 x 3 inch for appetizer size. Place on a baking sheet and brush with egg yolk. Refrigerate, uncovered, for 30 minutes. Reserve leftover puff pastry sheet for another use.

Preheat the oven to 375°F. Bake for 15 minutes until golden and crisp. Place a ramekin or metal cutter in each corner of the baking tray with the pastry and simply rest a second baking sheet on top. This may all sound complicated, but I promise you it isn't, and you will see the benefit of restaurant-quality millefeuille once the pastry is cooked. Once it is out of the oven, allow it to cool thoroughly.

Meanwhile, warm the oil in a saucepan over a low heat. Add the shallots, garlic, and rosemary until soft and translucent. Now increase the heat to medium and add the mushrooms, stirring well to cook through lightly. Add the Madeira, salt and pepper and simmer for 2 minutes.

In a separate saucepan, bring the cream to a simmer, then pour over the chocolate in a heatproof bowl, whisking well.

To assemble the millefeuille, using a serrated knife, slice through each pastry rectangle twice horizontally to give you three thin layers from each. Place the bottom layer on the serving plate and carefully add some of the mushroom mixture, followed by some of the chocolate sauce. Repeat for the next layer.

Drizzle some of the chocolate sauce around each finished millefeuille, then add a scattering of chives and a drizzle of olive oil.

# Cacao-nib-crusted halibut with sautéed spinach and wild mushrooms

This recipe comes from one of my close friends, Alan Jones, a highly skilled chef based close to my Islington shop. The dish is stunning and perfect for dinner parties. It takes a little while to prepare, but there are times when you need to wow your guests with your culinary and presentation skills.

## FOR THE COCOA-NIB CRUST

5 slices of white bread

¼ cup packed fresh flat-leaf parsley

2 ounces Comté cheese

4 tablespoons unsalted butter, softened

2 tablespoons cocoa nibs

## FOR THE HALIBUT

4 fillets of wild Scottish halibut (about 5 ounces each), trimmed of skin and grey fat

Sea salt and freshly ground black pepper

## TO FINISH

9 ounces wild mushrooms (preferably morels and chanterelles)

12 ounces leaf spinach, stemmed

2 tablespoons unsalted batter, divided

Sea salt and freshly ground pepper

First, make the cacao-nib crust. Remove the crusts from the bread and cut each slice into quarters. In a food processor, blend the bread and parsley together for about 1 minute. Then add the cheese, followed by the butter, and blend until a smooth green paste is formed. Finally, add in the cocoa nibs and pulse to combine. Roll out between 2 pieces of waxed paper to about ¼ inch thick. Refrigerate until firmly set.

Preheat the oven to 350°F.

Remove the hardened cocoa-nib paste from the fridge with the paper still on, lay all the halibut pieces on top. Cut around each piece of fish, leaving a small margin of extra crust on all sides. Remove the paper and place a piece of the crust on top of each halibut fillet.

Transfer the crusted fish onto a baking sheet lined with parchment paper and bake for 6–7 minutes. To check whether the fish is cooked through, gently insert a wooden toothpick into the thickest part of the fish: if you do not feel any tension it is ready.

While the fish is cooking, separately sauté the mushrooms and spinach in the butter. Season with salt and pepper, then briefly drain on kitchen towels. Place the spinach in the centre of a warm bowl with the wild mushrooms in a ring around it, then simply place the cooked fish on top. Serve immediately.

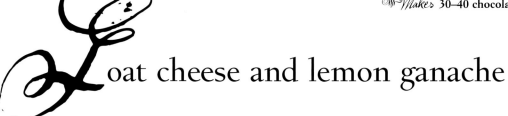

# oat cheese and lemon ganache

Goat cheese isn't the most obvious food to pair with chocolate, but when lemon is introduced the result is to die for – similar to cheesecake but with a slightly more acidic finish and a lighter texture. Be sure to use an excellent, preferably local rindless soft goat cheese. If you can find it, use a goat fromage blanc, best-quality cream cheese is a good alternative. The ganache makes very addictive chocolates, but also tastes wonderful spooned over frozen summer berries.

**9 ounces rindless plain goat cheese**

**4 ounces goat fromage blanc or cream cheese**

**Juice and zest of 2 lemons**

**1 cup organic sugar**

**14 ounces white chocolate, chopped**

**About 40 chocolate shells and tempered chocolate, if desired**

Bring $1/2$ cup water to a simmer with the goat cheese, fromage blanc, and lemon zest and juice, and simmer until smooth. Add the sugar and stir well, then add the chocolate and whisk until smooth. Taste the ganache and adjust the sugar if necessary. Let cool and pipe into dark chocolate shells of your choice, or refrigerate and once set, use to roll into truffles.

# Sweet roasted green garlic ganache

I'm fascinated about pairing vegetables with chocolate, as there are so many aromatic, sweet, tangy, juicy, and textural vegetables that can work well with either sweet or savory flavors. The most challenging aspect of this ganache is to incorporate green garlic without its being acrid and overwhelmingly pungent. It takes time to prepare, but for an unusual and savory chocolate the results will astound you. Young green garlic, which is not to be confused with mature supermarket garlic, is available in farmer's markets in the spring. It looks like a bulbous scallion with a soft, not flaky skin. The ganache can be used as a savory sauce, or try using it to fill shells for an interesting savory chocolate which goes amazingly well with cheese and pickles.

**1 bulb of young green garlic**

**1 tablespoon walnut oil**

**1¼ cups organic sugar**

**1 pound 66% dark chocolate, chopped**

**6 tablespoons heavy cream**

**About 40 chocolate shells and tempered chocolate, if desired**

Preheat the oven to 300°F.

Place the green garlic onto a baking sheet and rub well with the walnut oil to coat fully. Bake for 1 hour. After that time, check the bulb to see how soft and caramelized it has become – it should be dark and very soft. If not, leave it in the oven until fully caramelized (the cooking time can vary depending on the garlic's size and freshness).

Once cooked, let the garlic cool thoroughly. Remove all the tough dry skins. You should be left with a glorious mound of golden garlic. Now pass this through a sieve using the back of a spoon or a spatula to remove all the fibers and remaining skin. You should now have a smooth paste.

To make the ganache, bring 1¾ cups of water to a boil in a saucepan with the sugar, pour over the chocolate in a heatproof bowl and whisk well. Add the garlic, 1 teaspoon at a time, until you reach a strength you are happy with. Let infuse for 30 minutes. Whisk in the cream, which will help to smooth the flavors and help emulsify the ganache. Let cool, then pipe into shells or refrigerate until set and then use to roll into truffles.

# Marmite truffles

You will either love this ganache or hate it, just as many people have a love-hate relationship with Marmite. It took two months of careful experimenting to get this recipe well balanced and palatable without its losing its distinctive tangy, salty edge. The ganache is so soft that it cannot be rolled, and if available use shells made from Madagascan chocolate as it has just enough acidity to balance with the marmite.

1 small jar of Marmite

1 quart spring water

2½ cups organic sugar

1 pound Madagascan 64% dark chocolate, chopped

About 40 chocolate shells and tempered chocolate, or cocoa powder, as desired

Put the Marmite, water, and sugar in a saucepan, bring to a boil and simmer for 3 minutes. It is very important to do this in order to slightly mellow the flavor of the Marmite. Pour over the chocolate in a heat proof bowl. Emulsify in a blender for 30 seconds. Allow to cool before using to fill shells, or leave to set in the fridge and then hand roll truffles. This ganache will last for 2 weeks if refrigerated.

# Caramelized red-onion and rosemary truffles

Just as pungent as garlic, onion needs lots of long and gentle cooking to reduce the volatile acids and overpowering compounds. Use the ganache to fill chocolate shells, or try spreading it on a pizza base and then top with mascarpone, chicken, and fresh basil.

3 tablespoons olive oil

1 large sprig of rosemary

1 teaspoon Maldon sea salt

2 medium red onions, peeled and very thinly sliced

1 cup light muscovado sugar

1 pound 67% dark chocolate from the Dominican Republic, chopped

Heat the oil, rosemary and salt in a frying pan over low heat. Add the onion and cook, stirring well, until reduced, dark golden and very, very soft. This can take up to an hour. Do not try to rush the process by turning the heat up or the sugars in the onion will over-caramelize and become bitter. Now remove the rosemary and push the onion pulp through a sieve. You will be left with an onion purée.

Bring 1³/4 cups water to a simmer with the sugar, then pour over the chocolate in a heatproof bowl and whisk to emulsify. Now mix in the onion purée. Let cool and thicken slightly, mixing well to distribute the onion through the liquid.

# Chocolate dressings for salads, fish, and ice cream

There is something special about real-chocolate vinegars or dressings, either to give as presents in a beautiful bottle or to use in your daily cooking. They add a luxurious and indulgent feel to salads, pasta dishes, fish, and meat, and can taste great with ice cream, too.

## Chocolate vinegar

This chocolate balsamic vinegar works wonderfully with salads, fish, and ice cream. You can adapt the recipe to use all sorts of other vinegars, including sherry vinegar, cider vinegar, raspberry vinegar, and even rice wine vinegar. And you can play around with different types of chocolate, too. If you are using balsamic vinegar, it makes a huge difference to the flavor if you use the authentic stuff made in Modena, Italy; avoid the cheap versions flavored with caramel.

⅔ cup balsamic vinegar

½ cup organic sugar

2 ounces African 85% dark chocolate, chopped

Simmer the vinegar and sugar in a saucepan until the sugar has dissolved fully. Add the chocolate and mix well. Let cool, then use to drizzle, pour, and garnish.

## Salad dressing

Why not reinvent your salads by using a chocolate dressing to finish off either a warm or a cold salad? The recipe below, which is remarkably easy to make, is based on the recipe for chocolate vinegar, but feel free to add any additional flavors that take your fancy. Try the dressing on warm green vegetables or pasta, or drizzled over focaccia.

All you need to do is measure 6 tablespoons chocolate vinegar into a jar or bowl, then add 3 tablespoons olive oil and shake or whisk vigorously until emulsified. Of course, you can adapt the quantities to suit. Add salt and freshly ground black pepper to taste.

# Vinegar ganaches

There are two methods for creating a vinegar ganache, and you can use either for balsamic, sherry, cider, fruit or rice wine vinegars. One method involves cooking the vinegar, which mellows and tempers the acidity; the other avoids cooking the vinegar, which creates a more vibrant and mouthwatering ganache.

# Balsamic vinegar ganache

**1 cup aged balsamic vinegar, preferably from Modena**

**1 cup organic sugar**

**Pinch of sea salt**

**14 ounces Madagascan 64% dark chocolate, chopped**

Boil the balsamic vinegar in a saucepan over a medium heat and reduce by half. In another saucepan, bring $1^{1}/_{3}$ cups water to a simmer with the sugar and a pinch of sea salt. Pour over the chocolate in a heatproof bowl and whisk well. Now add the reduced vinegar and mix thoroughly. Let cool before tasting. The flavor will be mellow and smooth, not at all acidic.

# Rice wine vinegar ganache

**1¼ cups organic sugar**

**Pinch of sea salt**

**18 ounces fine 66% dark chocolate, chopped**

**1 cup rice wine vinegar**

Bring $^{2}/_{3}$ cup water to a simmer with the sugar and salt. Pour over the chocolate in a heatproof bowl and blend. Now add the vinegar without any cooking at all. Let cool and then taste. The flavor will be much more acidic, clean, and very astringent – a very good palate-cleanser.

# Resources

## Suppliers

**British ingredients, such as golden syrup, Maldon salt, and Marmite**
www.britishfoodshop.com
www.britshoppe.com

**Cake boards, powder colors, cake boxes and decorations**
www.sugarcraft.com
www.amazon.com
www.shopbakersnook.com
www.pastrysampler.com

**Chocolate and ingredients**
www.chocolatepath.com
www.worldwidechocolate.com
www.bridgewaterchocolate.com
www.chocosphere.com
www.deandeluca.com

**Chocolate molds and equipment**
www.candymoldcentral.com
www.chocolateworld.be
www.chocolatemachine.com
www.getsuckered.com
www.streichs.com

**Chocolate molds, packaging and couverture**
www.homechocolatefactory.com

**Chocolate truffle shells**
www.hauserchocolates.com

**Edible gold**
www.ediblegold.com

**Herbs and essential oils**
www.iherb.com

## Paul A. Young Fine Chocolates

143 Wardour Street
Soho
London W1F 8WA
+44 (0)20 7437 0011

33 Camden Passage
Islington
London N1 8EA
+44 (0)20 7424 5750

20 The Royal Exchange
Threadneedle Street
London EC3V 3LP
+44 (0)20 7929 7007

www.paulayoung.co.uk

## Acknowledgments

I would like to thank my mum and Kevin for all the years of support and guidance; my grandma for all the baking days of my childhood, as well as Auntie Brenda and Uncle Mike, Louise Vaughan and Stuart Silvers.

Thank you to my business partner James Cronin for his amazing hard work and for believing in my dreams; Kate Johns, my PR, for five years of fabulous support; Rob Common, my agent; my loyal and hard-working team; all my family and friends for their support and encouragement; Kyle Cathie and her amazing team, especially Jenny Wheatley and Emily Hatchwell for being so understanding and patient; and Anders Schønnemann,

Carl Hodson, Annie Rigg and Tabitha Hawkins for helping to create this gorgeous book. And of course, all my loyal customers.

I would also like to thank Rik Gadsby, the Academy of Chocolate, Roger Pizey, Tim Payne, Marco Pierre White, Paul Whitehouse, Nigella Lawson, Angus Deayton, Lise Mayer (and Isaac), Jeni Barnett, Tom Moggach, Sara Jayne-Stanes, Hardeep Singh Kholi, Lotte Duncan, Lydia Slater, and every journalist who has written encouraging and enlightening articles about us.

Additional thanks to Tricia Cronin, Anna Cronin, Frances Openshaw and New College Durham, Kirt Holmes,

James Gardiner, Andrew Nutter, Ruth and Mike Sandys-Edwards, Shona, Rupert and Imogen Hancock, Rosalind Rathouse, Terry Laybourne, Clare Handford, Sir Alan Sugar and the *Apprentice* production team.

Thank you to all my loyal suppliers including Valrhona, Amedei, Michel Cluizel, Seasoned Pioneers, Lewis Dairies, Kings Fine Foods, Pod, Wrapology, la Cave à Fromage and Groovy Train web design.

And finally to Velcro, my gorgeous basset hound, for being the best de-stressing and relaxing thing in my life.

# Index

Page numbers in **bold** refer to photographs.